house beautiful

gardens

DESIGN PRINCIPLES AT WORK OUTDOORS

THE EDITORS OF HOUSE BEAUTIFUL MAGAZINE

LOUIS OLIVER GROPP

Editor in Chief

MARGARET KENNEDY

Editor

TEXT BY

SUZANNE CHARLÉ

HEARST BOOKS

NEW YORK

www.williammorrow.com

Library of Congress Cataloging-in-Publication Data

House Beautiful gardens : design principles at work outdoors /
    by the editors of House Beautiful.
            p.   cm.
    ISBN 0-688-15103-5
    1. Landscape gardening. 2. Gardens—Design. I. House
beautiful.
SB473.H64   1998
712—dc21   98-3939
                                                    CIP

PRINTED IN SINGAPORE

First Edition

10   9   8   7   6   5   4   3   2   1

EDITOR
JOHN SMALLWOOD

ART DIRECTOR
TOMEK LAMPRECHT

PRODUCED BY SMALLWOOD & STEWART, INC., NEW YORK

c o n

FOREWORD   8

INTRODUCTION   10

PART I

points of view   14

PART II

the garden deconstructed   90

ENTRANCES   92
INSIDE/OUT: PORCHES & PATIOS   98
WALLS & HEDGES   106
FENCES & GATES   114
PATHS & STEPS   122
ALLÉES, PERGOLAS & ARCHES   130
WATER   136

tents

SUMMER HOUSES
& OTHER STRUCTURES 144
OBJECTS 150
SEATS 156

PART III

garden + house 162

SITE GARDENS 164
PERFECT UNIONS 176

DESIGNER DIRECTORY 204

PHOTOGRAPHY CREDITS 206

f o r e w o r d

On a balmy May afternoon when I was nine, giddy from the scent of the two dozen lilac bushes in my grandmother's garden, I tumbled blissfully down a grassy slope. At that moment, I realized how magical a garden can be. After my grandmother died, my family moved to her house. Though I loved racing around the neatly edged flower beds brimming with poppies, phlox, and soaring delphiniums, I was not up for endless weeding. Three young children plus a job soon forced my mother to throw in her trowel and each summer I despaired as another rectangle reverted to lawn. Finally nothing remained except hydrangeas, a few clusters of peonies, one unstoppable old rose, and of course, the lilacs.

Now I am gardening—in pots on a city terrace and on two country acres each weekend. My ambitions exceed both my available hours and budget, and I'm constantly revising. Whether visiting gardens or pouring over photographs for a layout, I continually look for inspiration. From the artful gardens published in *House Beautiful*, I've lifted many a creative solution, transplanting another gardener's ploy to my own plot. This book compiles the best of those seductive ideas and bulges with wisdom, visions, and answers each of us can apply to our own corner of this Earth.

Serendipitously, my house in the country came with masses of old lilacs, and my mother dug up some of *her* mother's peonies, which now thrive for a grateful granddaughter. Some of the pieces are in place, yet I'm still struggling to connect the dots on my garden plan. But I have learned to appreciate the merits of weeding—it does, after all, keep us in the garden.

MARGARET KENNEDY

EDITOR

n recent years, the garden and what it means to Americans—its very definition—has experienced a revolutionary, some might say radical, change. Drive through any suburb and you will see the signs: What was once a predictable, even monotonous expanse of green lawn bound to the house by foundation plantings has fragmented into cottage gardens that reach out to the curb, planned jungles of vines, ornamental grasses and lilies tangled with precision, and geometric paved terraces masquerading as driveways. In one village—Seaside, Florida—grass sod has even been outlawed in favor of native plants, luxuriant boscages of oak, Southern magnolia, and beach rosemary.

At the turn of the 21st century, our gardens are as diverse as our population, taking inspiration from civilizations as disparate and remote as ancient Persia and China and receiving wisdom from the scientific findings of global ecologists. A garden can be a modern ode to the 17th-century designer André Le Nôtre, composed of allées, bosquets, clipped hedges, and *tapis vert*, or it can be a seemingly natural meadow of wildflowers skillfully shaped by an unseen hand.

In large part, this expanded definition is the result of our greater access to an unprecedented array of plants and information on the propagation, design, and history of gardens. It also comes from a willingness to accept, even an enthusiasm to embrace, different points of

view. The ties that linked a particular period of history to a particular style of gardening have been broken: In our gardens, as in our multicultural society, an energetic, if sometimes confusing, eclecticism reigns.

This eclecticism has encouraged a highly personal approach to gardening, one that allows the gardener to explore idiosyncratic visions and to express singular enthusiasms and dreams. It is the garden as journal, as autobiography, as private creation myth. It is no longer defined by a shared, dominant taste. One need only turn to the story on the successful garden that appeared in a 1912 issue of *House Beautiful* to realize how different things were when Style was capitalized: Aside from the caption, there is nothing to suggest that the sunnily mundane park in the accompanying photo had once been owned by Lord Byron, the Romantic poet who made high art of defiance and melancholy. One can't help but wonder what brooding, mysterious landscape the sardonic author of *Don Juan* would compose today.

The gardens in this book *are* that transparent, offering horticultural clues to the passions and personalities of the creative spirits who planned and planted them. Varying in locale, size, and style, the only thing these gardens have in common is that they are all the works of "mad keen gardeners," a term coined by one of the breed's keenest, Christopher Lloyd.

Amongst this complex society are consummate collectors such as James David, whose passion for finding plants that thrive in the harsh Texas environment is equalled only by his love of high-maintenance gardening. In Connecticut, Michael Trapp uses the Smiths and Joneses of the horticultural world—plants typically despised as commonplace by "serious" gardeners—in quixotic combinations and sheer numbers to conjure up otherworldly tableaux. (Picture a flock of ostrich ferns running, shoulder high, into a copse, or a mid-summer flag-day display of a hundred hollyhocks and you have a glimpse of his vision.) Frank Cabot searches the world and history for exotic vegetation and architecture; Jim Thompson is content to stick with one plant—heather—exploring with a dedication verging on the obsessive the ways in which its various colors and hues can be combined.

In portraying these gardens, we hope to suggest some of the diverse paths people have chosen to mold and tame their particular pieces of Earth. Each individual has considered the special circumstances of his or her garden—the location, the number of hours to be dedicated to the work at hand, how the land is to be used, the budget—and has designed accordingly, sometimes painstakingly drafting plans, other times responding intuitively on site to some prodding muse or rude necessity. Each gardener has tried and with some plants failed and tried again, recognizing that much of the joy in gardening and many of the psychic rewards come in the doing of it: digging in the dirt, smelling the flowers, sharing knowledge and plants with other enthusiasts. Each and every one of these gardeners knows full well that mistakes as well as triumphs are necessary steps in the evolution of a numinous landscape, one's own personal Eden.

PART I

points of view

urban inspiration

Ben Page's trip to Mexico inspired experiments in color and texture (opposite). Yellow sunflowers grow next to pink oriental lilies in front of wisps of feather reed grass. Page's formal layout for his small urban garden (above) gives it seasonal strength, so that it is interesting even in winter.

L ANDSCAPE ARCHITECT BEN PAGE GREW UP PLAYING IN HIS GRAND-mother's and great-grandmother's huge perennial gardens in rural Kentucky. And so when he and his wife, Libby, bought a house in downtown Nashville, their first garden was a small replica of the informal English-style gardens of his youth.

But soon they realized that their garden needed to evolve. Perennial gardens are delights during spring and early summer, but in the depths of winter can look pretty grim. Since the Pages' garden is so close to the house, what Ben called "the ugly period" was particularly disheartening. He set about redesigning the site with a honeycomb of brick paths and stone

terraces to give the garden seasonal strength, as well as to make it a more pleasurable place to entertain—something the family does regularly.

In his designs for clients, Page devises landscapes that reveal themselves slowly, building a sense of enticement, of mystery. Never an easy task, such a sleight of hand was a particularly tall order for his own small lot, just 75 by 100 feet. And yet he managed brilliantly. To hide the corner garden from the street, Page built an eight-foot-high masonry wall, green with ivy and topped with fanciful ironwork. To enter, guests must pass through a heavy wooden gate into a 10-by-10-foot "decompression chamber," which, Page said, helps friends "get into a garden mood." Walled with arborvitae and paved with black, white, and pink river stones, the

Tennessee Crab Orchard stone surrounds the fountain (above). The wall is screened by 'Flying Dragon' trifoliate orange, a pygmy flowering dogwood, and 'Firecracker' witch hazel. Arborvitae and a Gothic Revival–inspired arch (opposite) separate the main garden from the quiet, mosaic-paved "entrance hall," with its subdued palette of grays and greens.

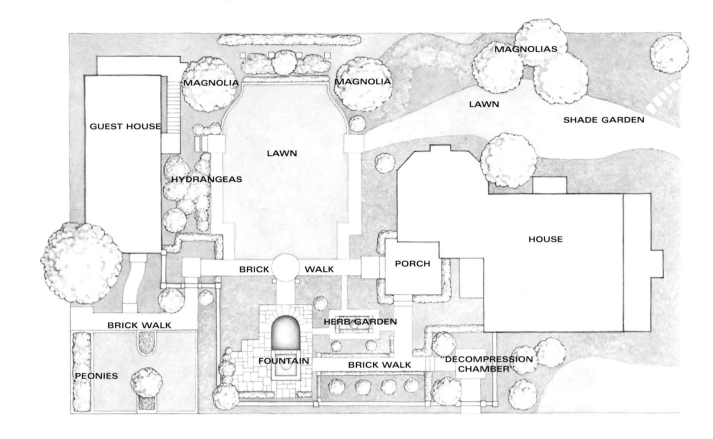

In the plan, labels read:

MAGNOLIAS

MAGNOLIA   MAGNOLIA

LAWN

GUEST HOUSE

SHADE GARDEN

LAWN

HYDRANGEAS

HOUSE

BRICK   WALK   PORCH

BRICK WALK

HERB GARDEN

PEONIES

FOUNTAIN   BRICK WALK   "DECOMPRESSION CHAMBER"

In spring, the structure of the herb garden is evident (opposite). Three kinds of lettuce and three types of rosemary line the rectangle, while golden-leaved geraniums anchor the corners. Pots contain lcmon and grapefruit trees that winter inside; white roadside daisies reseed themselves every year. To the rear, the wall is a tangle of two kinds of climbing honeysuckle ('Alabama Crimson' and 'Lime Tart'), climbing roses ('Old Blush' and 'Cécile Brunner'), and clematis.

"entry hall" has as its signature piece a diminutive weeping kousa dogwood. "It's just like putting your best piece of porcelain or a fine Aubusson in the central entry hall," the landscape architect explained. Here, one is allowed only a glimpse of the main garden, but the whisper of the nearby fountain, the scent of the neighboring roses, hint at what is to come.

Every inch counts in the Pages' garden: Off the car park, in a private "back" entry, an extensive collection of evergreen hellebores is massed against the wall; close by is a rare form of redbud called the Texas white redbud. Just outside of the house are an herb garden and a parterre, delineated by a narrow herringbone brick path that transmutes to pea gravel, changing a stroller's pace and sense of place. These paths lead to a square brick pool, with a single jet of water, and a U-shaped goldfish pond. Named Florence's Garden for the Pages' daughter, who often plays here with her friends, the small space provides axial vistas of the garden.

Page refused to be limited by the size of the lot, either in the number of sections of the garden or in the eclectic and multi-textured plant material, which ranges from friends' "pass-along" plants and daisies found on the roadside to Egyptian papyrus and a rare pygmy flowering dogwood. "I try to push as hard as I can," he said.

contained freedom

The New England spring arrives with a fanfare of 15 varieties of tulips (opposite), including an old favorite, 'Spring Green', and more recent entries, 'Lilac Perfection' and 'Queen of Night'. The cypress picket fence that surrounded the 40-by-100-foot garden echoed the cedar clapboard house, while the gray granite base referred to the stone foundation. The sunroom of the original farmhouse overlooked the enclosed garden (above), where brick paths repeated the flooring pattern.

T IS A SAD STORY WITH A HAPPY ENDING: AFTER SEEING A WALLED GARDEN designed by Nancy McCabe, Pamela Logan asked her good friend to create an enclosed garden that would look as if it had always nestled next to the 18th-century New England farmhouse Pam shared with her husband, Peter.

Using the enclosed gardens of the Middle Ages as her inspiration, McCabe designed a 30-by-60-foot rectangle, divided into four vegetable and six flower beds that were defined by brick paths and a picket fence. The strict demarcations laid the groundwork for a surprisingly forgiving design, which allowed Logan to plant freely, and not worry whether a plant was tall or short. In midsummer she was rewarded with an exuberant, and very personal, mass of colors, textures, and shapes. "I'm no Penelope Hobhouse," Logan freely admitted. The design took that into account.

Logan and McCabe, both garden-history buffs, enjoyed deciding which new variety of tulips to put in the flower beds, which heirloom herbs to plant in the vegetable plot, the best sites for the espaliered apple and pear trees. To keep the garden in tune with its Maine surroundings, McCabe used granite to form the base of the enclosing wall, which matched the granite foundation of the house, and topped it with a cypress fence that quickly aged to gray, matching the cedar clapboard of the house. Paths of old bricks were laid in a variety of traditional patterns, gracefully referring to the brick floor of the sun porch; old mill stones collected by the previous owner were used as accents. As a finishing touch, McCabe commissioned Phyllis Palmer, a New York artist, to cast in bronze a menagerie—owl, rabbit, frog, turtle, bushy-tailed squirrel—of amiable guardian spirits to perch atop fence posts.

And then the old house burned down. But Logan was not deterred: Today, a new cedar-shake house with large French doors forms a 'U' around

the garden: "The new design takes much better advantage of the garden," she said. "Old houses are basically inward looking; this one is totally oriented to the outside."

Well aware of Maine's short growing season, in early June Anthony Elliott of Kennebunk's Snug Harbor Farm fills in the spaces around the perennials with bright annuals straight from the greenhouse.

Originally, the kitchen garden had a bright palette—reds and yellows—while the flower garden was composed predominantly of purples, pinks, and whites, with a few pale yellows thrown in: roses, tulips, holly-hocks, dianthus, astilbes, lamb's-ears, clematis. Now that the garden is embraced by the house, Logan is adding more reds and yellows that demand attention. She has also planted more fragrant flowers such as heliotrope, peacock orchid, and three kinds of nicotiana ('Lansdorfii', 'Sylvester', and 'Alata'—which smell best after dusk): "I have always loved the sweet smells in the evening," she commented. Now those scents will waft into every room.

A pale double tulip called Angelique (above) adds delicacy to the garden. In the main flower bed (opposite), a profusion of annuals, including bachelor's-buttons, snapdragons ('Frost'), petunias ('Azure Pearls'), and sweet William, blooms until the first frost. The garden's structure is maintained by the foliage of perennials, including Siberian iris, lilies, peonies, and 'Taplow Blue' globe thistle, a plant much loved by the American goldfinch.

An old millstone forms the axis of the paths in the kitchen garden (opposite). Antique English forcing cloches nestle between rows of chives and red-leaved lettuces under an espaliered pear tree.

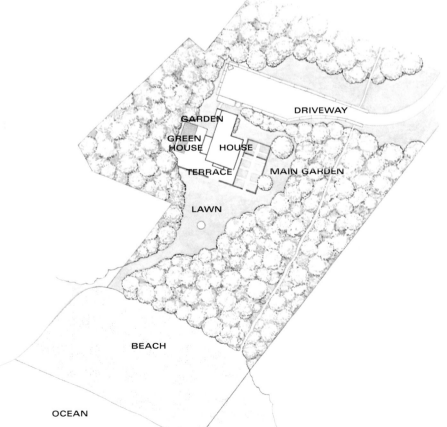

GARDEN

GREEN HOUSE

HOUSE

DRIVEWAY

TERRACE

MAIN GARDEN

LAWN

BEACH

OCEAN

Before the farmhouse burned down, Eddie, a bantam rooster, and his hen, Simone, were residents of a brightly colored chicken coop (above). The structure was moved during the construction of the Logan's new residence to its original home in Tony Elliott's nursery. Later it was moved to another friend's land. "You could call it a portable hen house," laughed Pam Logan.

Raymond Jungles mirrored the bold shapes and vibrant colors of his wife's murals with plantings of *Bambusa vulgaris* 'Vittata', golden Hawaiian bamboo, and Bismarck palm (opposite). Debra Yates' tile murals start in the house and stretch into the garden (above), connecting the inside to the outside, where a pot of *Vriesea imperialis* scents the air.

tropical eden

ALTHOUGH RAYMOND JUNGLES AND DEBRA YATES PRACTICE different disciplines—he is a landscape architect, she an artist—both approached the creation of their garden in Miami, Florida, with the same interests in mind: making the most of a lush tropical setting through composition, texture, and color.

"When we started, the garden looked like every other suburban-tract garden from the 1950s," said Jungles, who usually designs for estates and large-scale projects like the Ocean Reef Club. "Foundation planting, a few fruit trees, lots of vines and weeds."

Jungles cleared out most of these when he and his wife moved to the High Pines neighborhood just south of Coconut Grove. For privacy, he immediately started planting trees and building a fence around the perimeter of the 120-by-150-foot corner lot. Nothing special, just some field-grown *Sabal palmettos* (known locally as cabbage palm) and, for fencing, galvanized iron panels, chain-link, and 4-by-6-foot posts that were on sale at a nearby lumber yard. "The fence was kind of funky, but we painted it flat black and grew vines over it, so that it basically disappeared."

After that it was a 10-year process of accumulating cuttings and young plants, most of which have sculptural foliage: palms, cycads, orchids, bromeliads, and bananas are some favorites. Today, Jungles estimates that there are about 300 different species. Many are offspring from the garden of the late Brazilian artist and landscape designer Roberto Burle Marx, who was renowned for his passion for tropical plants and his powerful, abstract designs.

The influence of Burle Marx—who was a close friend of the couple and who stayed at the house on visits to the United States—is strikingly evident in the geometric ceramic murals that Yates designed for the garden. (Another of her bold murals is in the passenger terminal at Miami's international airport.) A 32-foot wall starts inside the house and stretches past the sliding glass doors into the garden, actually making the space look larger; another helps define the main area of the garden. In a splendid display of team work, Jungles picked up the colors of Yates' murals in his plantings, echoing the hot yellow with a clump of golden Hawaiian bamboo, and the vibrant reds and purples with banana flowers. Odd pieces of furniture, found in thrift stores, were painted in brilliant tropical colors.

Although the garden is carefully planned around the pool—with smaller patio areas spinning off of it, allowing people to sit in the sun or the shade—there is an underlying sense of chaos: "It is like a jungle, just barely cultivated," said Jungles. Plants are allowed to grow in their natural forms, requiring little pruning or clipping; grass between the paving stones is only occasionally cut. And while Jungles selected many of the plants, some arrived of their own accord as gifts from friends' gardens.

Even the elimination of plants was sometimes by chance: "The hurricane of '92 smashed and flattened the garden, but it was good—it opened up the garden," Jungles commented. A trellis that was blown over was succeeded by a tree house, and a neighbor's date palm that had been uprooted in the storm found a home in the couple's yard. "The garden is constantly evolving," he said. "It is our own personal Eden."

Making the most of Florida's climate, Jungles and Yates emphasized the sensuous shapes of tropical plants and their subtle color variations, including a banana flower (above), a bronze-leaved bromeliad, and variegated cream-and-green-striped Aztec grass (opposite above). The small garden is planted with 60 species of palm, including *Coccothrinax crinita*, or old man palm, from Cuba (opposite below).

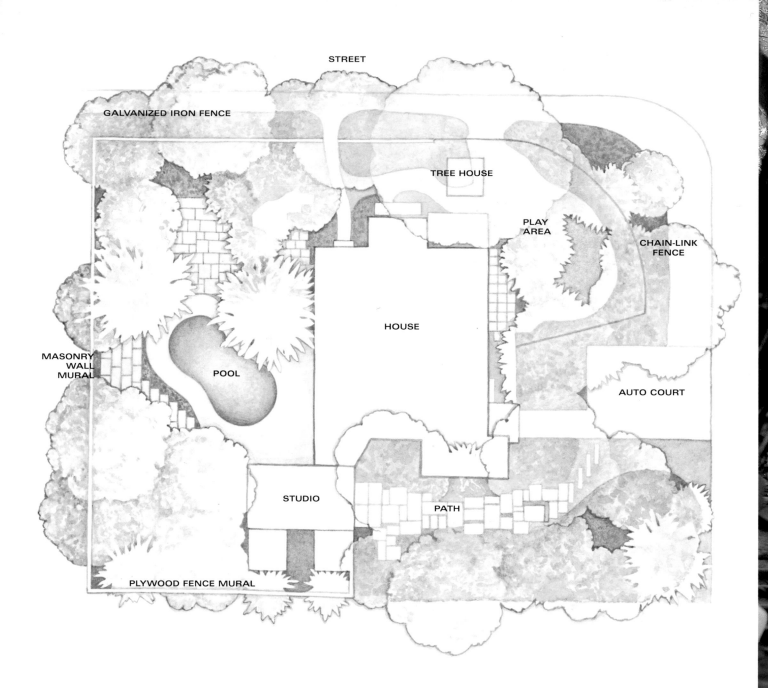

STREET

GALVANIZED IRON FENCE

TREE HOUSE

PLAY
AREA

CHAIN-LINK
FENCE

HOUSE

MASONRY
WALL
MURAL

POOL

AUTO COURT

STUDIO

PATH

PLYWOOD FENCE MURAL

A path makes its way
through the planned,
but just barely controlled,
suburban jungle of philoden-
dron, begonias, heliconias,
bananas, and yellow walking
iris, *Trimezia martinicensis*
(opposite). Like some of
the plants, the green and
gray concrete paving bricks
were castoffs, in this case
sample pieces from Jungles'
hotel projects.

bold strokes

A bark path leads from the house (opposite), where a sea of pachysandra glows in the overcast light, to the vegetable beds, potting shed, and greenhouse. Using a bright palette, the Osmuns planted red, pink, and white peonies and foxgloves; the border of blue fescue was raised from seed in the greenhouse. Sweeps of 'Moonlight' Scotch broom and a blue wave of ceanothus bloom in spring (above).

A VISIT TO EUGENIE AND WILLIAM OSMUN'S GARDEN ON Bainbridge Island in Washington at any time of year will provoke a similar response, though the vegetation is constantly changing. This is a garden of bold strokes, with sweeping bands of color: swaths of 'Moonlight' Scotch broom and bright yellow daffodils in the spring; brilliant whites of baby's-breath and daisies, and blues of ceanothus and lavender in the summer.

Knowing that William was a museum administrator before he retired, one suspects that a deliberate and referential artistry has guided the composition: This intensely modern garden looks as though it were inspired by the bold brushstrokes of a great 20th-century painter, Motherwell, perhaps, or Frankenthaler.

William rejects the suggestion: The approach, he declares, was as much by luck as by design. Some plants, like the lavender, took so well to the rich earth that they practically became invasive. 'Stella de Oro' daylilies are such happy residents that their burgeoning numbers have been continually dug up and planted elsewhere, forming new colonies.

The couple has no interest in the one-of-each gardening that appeals to some neighbors, preferring, instead, to plant in masses. The neighborhood, they feel, is too rural for anything overly manicured. Hence the use of wood bark for the broad paths, and kinnickinnick and pachysandra to cover the slopes. This approach also lends itself to fairly low maintenance, important since, until recently, the couple did all of the work in the garden themselves.

Eugenie and William Osmun had been gardening for many years by the time they bought the waterfront lot. But the Northwest landscape and vegetation was a world away from the walled terrace garden they had nurtured in Southern California. Gone were the begonias, the cymbidiums, the staghorn ferns: Here instead were 3½ acres of abandoned farmland,

Looking away from the house to the greenhouse (above, upper left corner), the circle garden in spring is awash in daffodils and the white blooms of Yakushimani rhododendron, chosen for its horizontal habit. William saved two old black locust trees, whose irregular bark remind him of the 19th-century illustrations of Arthur Rackham. A terrace off the large living area looks west to Puget Sound (opposite). In the summer, the trellis, twined with 'Interlaken' grapes, provides shade, but sunlight beams through in winter once the leaves have fallen.

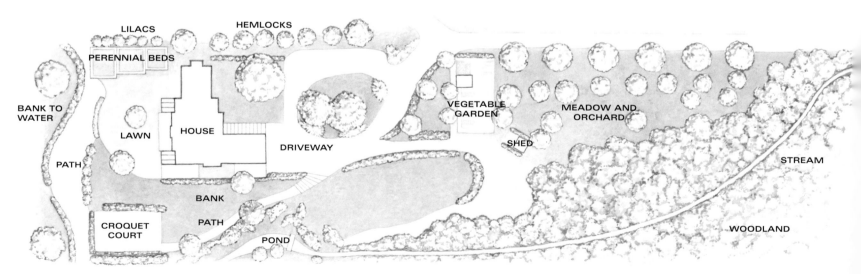

LILACS HEMLOCKS

PERENNIAL BEDS

BANK TO
WATER

LAWN HOUSE

VEGETABLE
GARDEN

MEADOW AND
ORCHARD

DRIVEWAY

SHED

STREAM

PATH

BANK

PATH

CROQUET
COURT

POND

WOODLAND

overrun with blackberries and dotted with a few old fruit trees. The couple left the woodland close to the road in its natural state, but they reclaimed the meadow, bulldozing the thicket of brambles. Near the precipitous, 50-foot drop to Puget Sound, the bulldozer worked the land, carving out one terrace for the new house and, lower on the slope, another for a croquet court.

Once the Osmuns moved into their house, planting began in earnest. In their plans, they divided the land facing the sound into three sections. A large, semi-circle swath of grass looped out from the house toward the water. This high expanse was anchored by two rectangles: one, the croquet court, down the slope and to the south, and framed by waves of David Austin English roses and lilies, Shasta daisies, 'Silver King' artemisia, baby's-breath, and English laurel; the other, three perennial beds to the north sheltered by a lilac hedge. "We didn't want to interrupt the view to the bay—we didn't want any distractions," said Bill.

The color scheme on the west is cool to match the blue and gray of the sound: blue, white, pale yellow. A sweep of 'Moonlight' Scotch broom—a demure version of bright yellow broom growing wild on the island—billows beside the cliff path that runs above the sound; swaths of baby's-breath and 'Hidcote' lavender succeed it later in the summer.

In the front of the house, a more intense palette predominates—white and brashly pink rhododendrons (Yakushimanum, 'Chionoides', 'Lem's Monarch'), and brilliant blue waves of ceanothus and Spanish bluebells break into a white foam of bishop's weed.

A path east to the working part of the garden—site of a greenhouse, potting shed, compost heap, fenced vegetable bed, and berry patch—is lined with, in succession, white, pink, and red peonies. Keeping an eye on costs, the Osmuns hesitated at planting these showy, fragrant flowers, until one catalogue offered large quantities at bargain-basement prices. The couple expanded the hot color palette with foxgloves and flamboyant oriental poppies, then underscored the hot colors with a blue line of fescue. Rather than purchasing the hundreds of plants necessary for such a design from a nursery, the couple bought a greenhouse and started their own seedlings—an investment that has aided them in subsequent grand sweeps of the imagination.

In the summer, mounds of baby's-breath glow beside a path leading west to the croquet court (opposite above), ringed with white Shasta daisies and 'Silver King' artemisia. A swath of evergreen 'Moonlight' Scotch broom, just to the rear, bloomed earlier in the spring. Behind the daisies a 10-foot-high laurel hedge abuts the neighboring woods. Just out of sight, a thorny hedge of gooseberries and *Rosa rugosa* 'Alba' keeps strollers away from a 50-foot drop to the sound.

multi-hued passion

Just outside the Thompsons'
living room, a "stained-
glass window" of heather
mimics the shape of the
house's glazing (opposite
and above).

TOURISTS TRYING TO REACH THE OCEAN NEAR THE SMALL TOWN OF Manchester, California, sometimes take a wrong turn and find themselves staring not at the Pacific, but at waves of purple, gold, and amber heather.

It is, no doubt, a surprise to find a sea of heather on the Northern California coast: The plants are native to Europe, and only one hybrid from the United States has ever been registered by the Heather Society in England. That plant, "Forty-Niner Gold," was cultivated by Jim Thompson, the man whose dedication, imagination, and luck brought this extraordinary landscape to life.

Jim, who as an Army colonel had never stayed in any place long enough to plant a garden, started this one over a decade ago, after his retirement and the chance purchase of a heather plant. The purchase was the beginning of a masterpiece. By using just one plant species, he could focus all his attention on a bold use of color. "All the colors harmonize—you can't make a mistake," Jim observed. When in doubt, he turns to his wife, who studied architecture at the University of California, Berkeley. ("He is color-blind," Beverley confided.) Whether Jim's modest claims are true or not, the result is a painterly vision.

The land, first cultivated in the mid-19th century by settlers whose dilapidated homestead hovers ghostlike at the edge of the 2½-acre site, was perfectly suited to heather, with its slightly acid soil (well drained but moist). The initial plants took so well that Jim and Beverley soon were ordering more. "I'd get one or two plants, make cuttings and reproduce them in a box," said Jim. Beverley, who grew up around gardens and gardeners in the Bay Area, took a more direct approach and stuck the cuttings right in the ground.

Both methods have worked superbly well. About 300 varieties cover ³/₄ of an acre in an undulating patchwork. Heathers—whether they belong to the genus *Erica*, *Calluna*, or *Daboecia*—grow to fairly uniform heights of 18 to 24 inches. In a particularly inspired bit of garden design, Jim created a rolling stage for the heathers, reshaping the pancake-flat land by digging trenches for paths and using the earth to form mounds of varying heights.

A preternaturally unassuming man, Jim explained that heather is the perfect plant for him: Once established, it requires no weeding and just a little mulching. Beverley gives the "haircuts."

August is the best time to see the garden, which is open to the public by appointment. But the garden of heather, with its variations in foliage and blooming times, is magical throughout the year—a color field fantasy with enchanting elements of childlike whimsy. Here, the gigantic limb of a Monterey cypress, bending to the ground, inspired a tree house: "The limb looked like a grand staircase," Jim recalled. He staked the trunk of another Monterey cypress at three points, transforming it into a sea dragon, writhing through a multi-hued sea of heather. (Beverley suggested a baby dragon to complete the family and Jim obligingly carved one out of

Previous page: Bordered by a wind break of shore pine (*Pinus contorta*), the heather garden includes the brilliant yellow *Erica cinerea* 'Golden Drop' and the silver-leaved *Calluna vulgaris* 'Silver Knight'. A path of pea gravel and wood (above), recycled from an old fence, meanders through the garden. 'Montgomery' Colorado spruce nestles in 'County Wicklow' heather (opposite above). Jim constructed a miniature patio (opposite below) of upended roofing shingles salvaged from the barn.

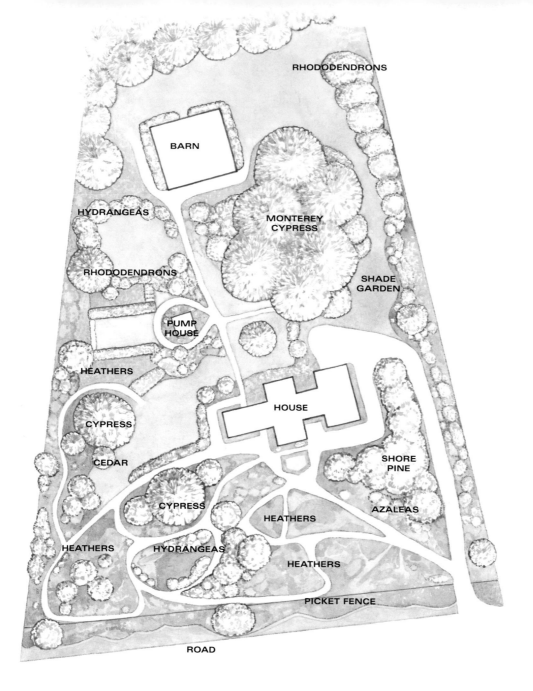

RHODODENDRONS

BARN

HYDRANGEAS

MONTEREY
CYPRESS

RHODODENDRONS

SHADE
GARDEN

PUMP
HOUSE

HEATHERS

HOUSE

CYPRESS

CEDAR

SHORE
PINE

CYPRESS

HEATHERS

AZALEAS

HEATHERS

HYDRANGEAS

HEATHERS

PICKET FENCE

ROAD

redwood.) Pieces of driftwood, finds from the couple's strolls on the beach, have their places in the garden as a bird bath, the base for a sundial, a bird house.

Such magic has cast its spell on others. Although Jim says that the most promising spots for growing heather in the United States are on the Pacific Coast, from Northern California up through Seattle, and on the East Coast, from Maryland to Maine, he and his wife have swapped information with gardeners in such unlikely places as Duluth, Minnesota, and Sweden. "I guess you just brush off the snow," said Beverley. "You might as well try."

Spikes of foxglove jut above waves of heather (opposite), including *Calluna vulgaris* 'Silver Queen', and, in the foreground, 'Long White'— the species from which Thompson took a mutant and cultivated 'Forty-Niner Gold.' At the edges of the garden, purple-flowered New Zealand tea trees make a colorful windbreak.

texas experiment

Between the gravel drive and limestone steps, flashes of vibrant zinnias (*Zinnia angustifolia*) thrive in the Texas heat while a barometer bush (*Leucophyllum frutescens*) beside the door creates the illusion of coolness (opposite). Nearby, a pergola entwined with blue trumpet flowers and white *Rosa* 'Popcorn' shade a terrace. Behind the house (above), orange cosmos trickle down the steps and Japanese persimmons fringe a small fish pond. Shells on the rim, construction-site finds, are fossilized reminders that Texas once lay beneath prehistoric seas.

Two decades ago, when James deGrey David and Gary Peese bought some two acres on the western outskirts of Austin, Texas, they wanted a garden suited to the region. Influenced by the environmental movement, David, a landscape architect, focused on the vegetation already growing on the scorched, west-facing site, augmenting it with plants native to the limestone hills and canyons of Central Texas, then adding semi-arid and tropical plants he found on his travels to Europe and Central and South America.

Spain and Mexico are inseparable from Texas history, and David refers to those cultures in his hardscape: An oval entrance terrace of local gravel and stone is enclosed by a stucco wall. Stone arches and walled terraces form a succession of gardens: A terrace of lawn and boxwoods hangs above

a terrace with sub-tropical plantings. On the lower, drier slope, native and desert vegetation find a home.

The hillside garden acts as a test site for varieties sold at Gardens, the nursery David owns with Peese. "The soil here, the plants, and to some extent the climate, are similar to those on the Mediterranean rim," David noted, but warned that he was not a purist. "The plant selection is very intuitive. I fall in love with some plants, I put them in the best possible situation. There will be one or two real survivors, and I build on those."

David believes that climate should dictate a garden's color palette: "Gertrude Jekyll's subtle pale pinks and lavenders work in misty England, but they're not effective in the Southwest." The bright Texas sun and the glare from the limestone hills washes out all but the most dynamic colors. And so, in one garden 'Durban' canna, a lily with festive foliage in shades of pink, orange, green, red, and purple, is backed by the red stems and leaves of Abyssinian bananas, which in turn are backed by towering green bamboos.

Pyramidal boxwoods and pots of herbs line a path dividing a bi-level vegetable garden (above left). A galvanized cistern collects run-off from the roof of the house to feed a system of ponds, basins, and channels. Walls and walks built with granite from local quarries underscore the garden's regional character (above right). 'Lady Banks' roses scramble on the cut blocks; black-foot daisies (*Melampodium leucanthum*) grow 6 feet tall in the interstices. A mid-level terrace doubles as dining area and service access (opposite).

Even more important than color are foliage, texture, and shape, since relatively few flowers bloom in the hot months of June, July, and August. On the main axis of the rear garden—which, unlike the organic plan of the front, is highly geometric—Italian cypresses stream down the hill toward the city, green and vertical; they are followed by a blue shadow of Arizona cypress, interspersed with tall red grass, *Pennisetum* 'Burgundy Giant', goldenrod, sunflowers, and a large rose bush, *Rosa chinensis* 'Mutabilis'.

The garden is under perpetual construction. "Three or four areas are always being intensely worked," David said, while the rest of the garden is allowed to establish itself. "I'd never recommend a garden like this for clients—I love high maintenance and I have help."

Off the dining room, Spanish grapevines shade a terrace studded with pots of clipped rosemary, holly, and box-wood. Behind the bench, on the southwestern slope, vegetation is much wilder, including Nelson's beargrass *(Nolina nelsonii)*, a West Texas native, and cacti that flourish in the full blast of the sun.

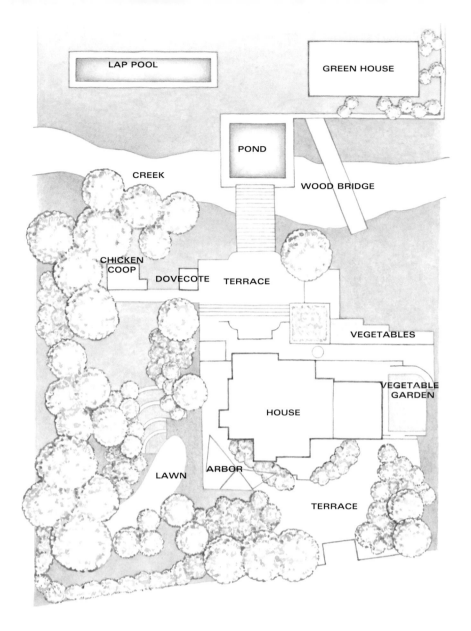

In one of the canyon's many micro-climates, variegated English ivy spills out of an urn (below), pulling the eye deep into a wooded area populated with hardy *Cleodendrum*, oakleaf hydrangea, crinum lily, iris, bamboo, ginger, and elephant's-ear *(Colocasia esculenta 'Antiquorum')*— all plants that thrive in the comparatively wet summer garden.

methodical madness

ADMIRERS OFTEN ASK MICHAEL TRAPP HOW HE DECIDED ON THE plan for his garden in West Cornwall, Connecticut. His answer, like the answer of all conjurers, is deceptively simple: He didn't. "After I bought the house, I was out of money," the antiquarian-cum-landscape designer recalled. "But I decided I could put down a few paths." He phoned a local gravel pit and a truck showed up and dumped 10 tons of riprap on his land. "Don't worry," the driver called out as he drove off. "I'll be back."

Thinking fast—and working with a determination born of necessity—Trapp turned 20 tons of hardscrabble into a rabbit's warren of paths, defining five major beds. Since then, necessity has metamorphosed into obsession: Single-handedly, the one-time landscape architecture student has reconfigured an entire street of cobblestones, some 78 tons, into paths, and done his best to deplete local quarries by erecting a maze of walls. "It's a very heavy garden," Trapp tossed off lightly.

Perched precariously on a steep promontory between a creek and the Housatonic River, the half-acre terraced garden gives the illusion of being much larger. Overgrown paths cross, vistas change suddenly, adroit adumbrations tantalize the stroller with secret charms of the unknown. Influences are European, of the far-away-and-long-ago variety: Trapp admires Italian classicism, English cottage gardens ("particularly the weird ones"), and the orderliness of French gardens. His catholic tastes show up in the myriad antiques that dapple the landscape—a Roman neoclassical fountain, a cast-iron balustrade from New Orleans, 18th-century Venetian volutes, olive oil urns from Crete and Spain. These objects impart a portentous sense of decaying antiquity—a neat act of deception considering that Trapp started the garden in 1991.

An irrepressible collector, Trapp chooses his plants much the way he

The view from Michael Trapp's bedroom: Sweet autumn clematis tumbles into the garden; *Rosa rugosa* 'Sir Thomas Lipton' and butterfly bush tangle in one of five beds. Palladian windows, once the glazing of the Rhode Island State House, help transform a garage into a summer house.

selects antiques: "I'll see something and think, 'Oh, that's good, that's unusual, it has a beautiful shape.' A plant is fine as long as it inspires you: I have no interest in a fascist approach, 'You must have a hot-and-cold border.' Who needs it?"

Although the plant population is decidedly commonplace—nepeta (also known as catmint), rugosa rose, lavender cotton, sunflowers—the combinations are not: Beds might be bordered with purple cabbages, drumstick allium, perhaps rosemary (never used for cooking). As summer approaches, a flock of ostrich ferns stretches, chin-high, into the distance. July is a kaleidoscope of color as 100 hollyhocks, 12 to 14 feet tall, bloom in concert. "It's like Alice in Wonderland," Trapp said with wonder, adding, "I like things out of context. Madness is my motif."

Objects are strewn throughout the garden like finds from some time-out-of-mind archeological dig. The main entrance (shutters from a New England church) is framed by Ionic columns and Spanish urns (above). A pair of urns from Crete mark a path on the lower terrace (opposite). A honeycomb of granite walls forms a grotto and terraces brimming with peonies, lily of the valley, and daylilies.

At the garden's central axis (opposite), towering Chinese junipers frame a mist-shrouded view of the far bank of the Housatonic River. On either side, butterfly bush and sunflowers capture the light; in the shadows, a marble neoclassical fountain feeds the reflecting pool, where elephant's-ears and chives grow. A lead lion mask from the Medici stable at the garden of Pratalino grimaces from its resting spot.

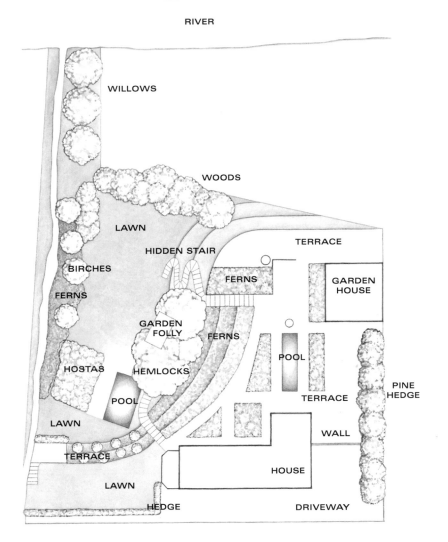

RIVER

WILLOWS

WOODS

LAWN

HIDDEN STAIR

TERRACE

BIRCHES

FERNS

GARDEN HOUSE

FERNS

GARDEN FOLLY

FERNS

POOL

HOSTAS

HEMLOCKS

TERRACE

PINE HEDGE

POOL

LAWN

WALL

TERRACE

HOUSE

LAWN

HEDGE

DRIVEWAY

A bust of Apollo (left), a memento of an 18th-century Grand Tour, floats in a flurry of ostrich ferns near a dead espaliered apple tree (pleased with the look, Trapp decided to leave it) and a Corinthian capital rescued from a 19th-century Ohio state insane asylum.

sea of grass

By early summer, fragrant Dutch lavender and *Sedum* 'Autumn Joy' crowd the steps leading from the terrace to the pool (opposite), and flowering stalks shoot up from *Yucca filamentosa* ('Adam's-needle'). Near the bay, tufts of fountain grass (*Pennisetum*) and clumps of giant Chinese silver grass (*Miscanthus giganteus*) stand up to the snows of January (above).

TODAY, THE OFFICES OF OEHME, VAN SWEDEN & ASSOCIATES ARE abuzz with 26 people working on 50 jobs. But in the early 1980s, it was just Wolfgang Oehme, a horticulturist from the University of Berlin, and James van Sweden, a landscape architect from the University of Michigan. The two had recently finished a job restoring the garden around the old Federal Reserve Annex, in Washington, D.C., when Alex and Carole Rosenberg contacted them about their summer house in Water Mill, Long Island, overlooking Mecox Bay. Private art dealers, the Rosenbergs gave the team carte blanche, asking only that the garden look as if it had always been there, and that the focus be the bay.

To make the most of the beauty of the bay, Oehme and van Sweden emphasized plants that seemed natural to the site—fountain grass, giant Chinese silver grass, and black-eyed Susan hybrids. They also planted Japanese black pine (*Pinus thunbergii*) to create a barrier against winds and neighboring houses. A rectangular vegetable, herb, and cut flower garden, enclosed with turkey wire in wood frames, was planted near the kitchen.

At the edge of the terrace off the house (opposite), a patch of yarrow grows in the shade of a weeping willow (*Salix babylonica*); beyond, a broad lawn sweeps to Mecox Bay and dense growths of common reeds (*Phragmites australis*). Overlooking the bay (above), the garden is a tapestry of greens, purples and yellows, including Japanese silver grass (*Miscanthus sinensis*), maiden grass (*Miscanthus sinensis* 'Gracillimus'), lavender, Russian sage (*Perovskia atriplicifolia*), fountain grass, and 'Coronation Gold' yarrow.

"We wanted the gardens to be soft, to blur into the natural edges," van Sweden remarked. Mindful of the nor'easters that sweep across the coast at 90 to 100 miles an hour, they kept the plant materials to a rather low height.

The stars are grasses and sedges—a dozen varieties planted in large masses. Tall and elegant, they subtly blend in with the grassy water reeds. A "balustrade" of *Pennisetum alopecuroides* frames the view of the bay from the terrace. By midsummer, purple-blooming Japanese silver grass and *Pennisetum alopecuroides* overhang the pool. Perennials—ligularia, well-loved by butterflies; coreopsis; and lavender—create an ever-changing tapestry. Discreet lighting at night emphasizes the architectural shapes of the plants.

Since the wild reeds, *Phragmites*, threatened to invade, the swath of lawn was kept large and geometric so that it could be cut frequently. Ease of maintenance was a key consideration for the grounds of this summer house: Once established, the grasses, which were chosen for their resistance to disease and pests in addition to their beauty, need watering only during the driest parts of the summer. On the exposed, sunny expanse, the spectacular plants shoot up, some 15 feet and taller, shading out weeds and requiring no pruning, staking, dead-heading, or other chores that might cut into more enjoyable summer pastimes.

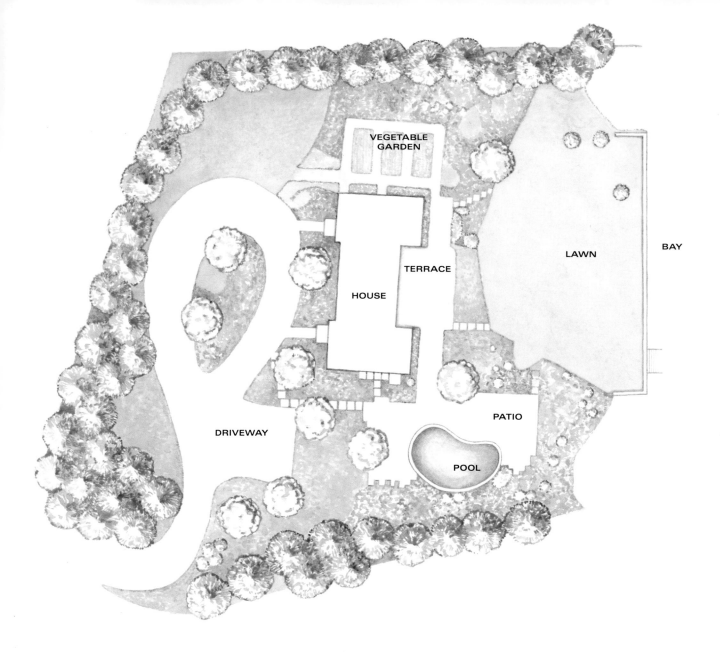

The only serious work in the garden comes in February, when the dried stalks from the previous year's growth are mowed, making way for the new; a mulch of shredded pine bark controls weeds and retains moisture. In early spring drifts of daffodils, alliums, and tulips pop through the stubble. These blooms are followed by drifts of flowering herbaceous perennials—yellow yarrow, lavender. In the advancing summer heat, the bouquet is expanded by Russian sage, a hybrid of native black-eyed Susan, and 'Autumn Joy' sedum. Toward the end of the summer, the grasses bloom: Maiden grass sprouts a silky plume, which becomes even more feathery, until finally the downy seeds are all released. It is a garden for all seasons, a sea of shimmering grasses that changes in color and intensity with the movement of the sun and clouds, just like the bay beyond.

In the summer, blue flowering spikes of Russian sage (above) are set off by the bright yellow blooms of 'Goldsturm' (left), a hybrid black-eyed Susan used liberally throughout the garden. A perennial with fuller, more intensely gold flowers than its American biennial roadside cousin, Goldsturm was popularized in the 1930s in Germany by Karl Soerster, one of the first modern proponents of ornamental grasses.

modern geometry

Broad, gradual terraces—punctuated by a half-unearthed boulder—frame a view of the early 20th-century farmhouse and a new addition, giving definition to the gentle slope (opposite). From the air, the formal/modernist approach becomes apparent, as does the heather "rug" garden (above).

A VISITOR TO THIS GEOMETRIC GARDEN ON A 2.6-ACRE CORNER lot in suburban Connecticut may not be surprised that the architect of the landscape, Richard Bergmann, is an admirer of André Le Nôtre. Less obvious, although equally important, is the influence of the 20th-century American landscape architect Dan Kiley, with whom Bergmann studied.

Like Le Nôtre, designer of such 17th-century gardens as Vaux le Vicomte and Versailles, Bergmann is interested in landscape as shaped and tamed by man, using hardscape to impose a formal geometry that is as striking in winter as in summer. Bergmann delights in creating *jeux d'esprit*: Improvising on what had been a half-circle fountain garden in a natural depression, the architect (who was schooled in both the Beaux Arts and the Modern traditions at the University of Illinois at Urbana) made a circular "rug" garden of heather. Planted in a cloverleaf, it is a "look-at" garden rather than a "walk-through" garden—a *parterre de broderie* providing amusing year-round patterns best viewed from the balcony off the master bedroom suite.

The earthwork and stonework envisioned by Bergmann were not for the faint of heart: A Midwesterner who was attracted to the East Coast in part because of its seasons, and in part because of its stone walls, Bergmann employed six stonemasons for four months. Using Connecticut fieldstones, the masons built a simulated drywall around the boundary of the corner property, homage to the old stone "fences" that traverse the Connecticut countryside. Bergmann rerouted a central driveway to the side of the property, turning a stand of trees into a natural gateway. A bold diagonal path, made of large flat stones from a local quarry, connects the drive to the farmhouse.

To define and formalize an insignificant slope that the architect says "was neither fish nor fowl," he planned a series of broad grass terraces, 15 feet wide, bound by stone edging. Originating as steps on the diagonal path, the stones turn at right angles toward the center of the property, disappearing into the slope only to re-emerge on the far side of the house, where they dissolve into a hemlock hedge. At ground level, the terraces insist that even the most casual stroller take note of the site gradations; from the air, they create a grand design, graphically tying the house to the landscape. Massive glacial rock outcroppings, which Bergmann carefully noted on a topographical map before beginning excavation, act as sporadic counterpoints to the strict geometry. (Unfortunately, the boulders' importance was not understood by the earth-moving contractor, who

A landscape for all seasons: In autumn, the fiery Japanese maple (above left) becomes a focal point, its "shadow" of fallen leaves mirroring the circular stone wall that encompasses the heather garden (above right). In winter, the stark black lines formed by evenly spaced stone terraces (opposite) shoot through the dappled pattern of snow on the diagonal walk, clearly defining the steps.

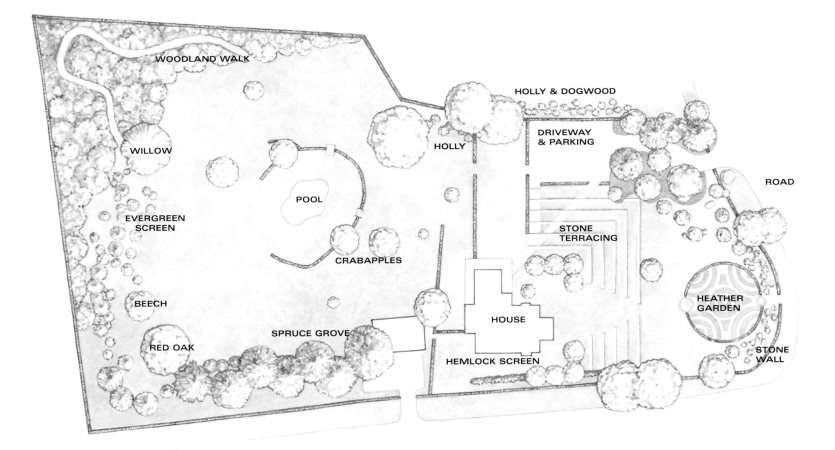

Labels on plan: WOODLAND WALK · WILLOW · EVERGREEN SCREEN · BEECH · RED OAK · SPRUCE GROVE · POOL · CRABAPPLES · HOLLY · HOLLY & DOGWOOD · DRIVEWAY & PARKING · STONE TERRACING · HOUSE · HEMLOCK SCREEN · HEATHER GARDEN · ROAD · STONE WALL

In the summer, Irish moss grows in the irregular spaces between the stones of the walk leading to the driveway (opposite), which is bound by a new fieldstone wall. A huge boulder—remnant of the last ice age—interjects itself into the formal geometry of the plan, becoming a natural point of divergence for the paths. Low-growing Japanese holly mimics the boulder's natural form.

went through great contortions to move some before the architect came to the site and stopped him.)

To block the view of a neighboring house on the far boundary, Bergmann imported a miniature forest of full-size eastern white pines; three types of spruce (Serbian, 'Montgomery' Colorado, and Norway); white fir; and string cypress; an evergreen tapestry inspired by a windbreak at the famed Connecticut nursery, White Flower Farm. A small grove of American holly, a special favorite of the owners, became an instant barrier near the intersection of the streets.

As for the influence of Dan Kiley, Bergmann says that he too prefers a structured approach to the garden, allowing the design—spare, formal, modern—to evolve out of the specific site. (In an informal tribute to his one-time instructor, Bergmann planted a small bosquet of 'Shade-master' locust near the front door and off the front sun porch.) In this architectonic landscape, the only flowering plants are old rose bushes and peonies, original to the site and relocated against a fence-topped wall that separates the formal front garden from the backyard dog run and play area, which remained much as it was originally. Aside from these flowers and the heather rug, the green palette prevails until autumn, when the scarlet leaves of Japanese maple and native dogwood blaze on the landscape.

In the wild garden (opposite), naturalized ox-eye daisies and daylilies, which bloom later in the summer, spread like a shadow under an old tree. In the misty distance, wetlands lead to Cooper's Neck Pond and, finally, to the Atlantic Ocean. A six-foot-wide mown grass path (above) curves through the 'Nikko Blue' bigleaf hydrangeas, then meanders along the perimeter of the meadow stretching to the house.

long island idyll

ROBERT MELTZER, A PRIVATE INVESTOR, BECAME PERSONALLY invested in gardening in 1987, when he and his wife bought a Colonial Revival house in Southampton, Long Island. With its meadows of wildflowers and native shrubs, a patch of woodland with stands of mature trees, a marshy expanse of wetlands, and a field gone wild with black locust and bittersweet, the 10-acre estate was a sort of physical digest of the various habitats of the coastal northeast. The possibilities excited Meltzer, who has made a career of spotting possibilities and taking advantage of them.

To get an idea of what they might do on the estate, Robert and Meryl visited Hidcote and other English gardens. But Robert decided that what he was seeing wouldn't work. "It was futile," Meltzer said. "Those gardens were appropriate to where they were. I wanted something that fit in Long Island."

He contacted A.E. Bye, a landscape architect based in Connecticut, whose subtle, elegant plan for the nearby estate of George Soros had caught Meltzer's attention. A master at understanding the essence of a landscape and bringing it out through the subtle manipulations of earth and native plants, Bye was just the person to recognize, revive, and enhance the natural strengths of the property.

With backhoe and bulldozer, Bye contoured the long flat stretch of meadow behind the house until it rolled and dipped like waves of the nearby Atlantic on a fair day. He planted trees and bushes that could withstand the salt spray of the sea, positioning them to the west so that at the end of a sunny afternoon, their shadows would play on the undulating lawn, welcome ephemeral guests. "Then he gave me courage to clear out the jungly undergrowth beneath the trees," Meltzer said, " and together we carved out a woodland path." Bye edited and simplified, exposing and emphasizing the structural beauty of vegetation and land.

But Meltzer wanted flowers, specifically old-fashioned roses, and Bye, whom Meltzer calls a "naturalist and minimalist," wasn't interested. "He thought a rose garden was a terrible idea, that it would be very hard to take care of," recalled Meltzer. So Meltzer approached designer Edwina vonGal.

The site chosen for the new rose garden was next to the tennis court. Rather than trying to hide the fence, vonGal transformed it into a rose arbor, and then repeated the fencing on the opposite side. She extended an existing hedge, creating four walls. "It became a rose room," said vonGal.

Meltzer was delighted, but he wanted to explore other types of gardens. And so, over the past seven years, Meltzer, vonGal, and Bye have continued their highly successful collaboration, working on other sections of the garden—what vonGal calls "Bob's events." "Bob is the gardener, I am the editor," commented vonGal. "Edwina gets me to focus on one project at a time," said Meltzer. "She gives structures to my ideas." Bye provides the underlying structure, bringing in a serpentine drive, screening the front property line with a stand of rhododendron, cotoneaster, and holly.

After clearing thickets of honeysuckle and bittersweet from the abandoned field behind the Meltzers' home, landscape architect A.E. Bye gently contoured the land. A mown path is the simple but effective separation between the grassy expanse and a new thicket of hundreds of hydrangeas and naturalized ox-eye daisies, privet, rose of Sharon, and spirea, all planted by Meltzer.

Hollyhocks grace the herb garden (opposite), where lavender, chives, and Russian sage thrive. In the spring, wide bands of nepeta line the grass walk in the rose "room" (above), and 'New Dawn' climbing roses ramble on the wire fence next to the tennis court; on the left, mahogany-colored bearded irises stand sentry in front of sweet-scented, old-fashioned shrub roses. A small tool shed, inspired by structures at Mount Vernon, serves as the focal point.

"What's so impressive about Bob's garden is that it is so large—that it covers all of that space, and yet manages to draw you in in a very nice way," commented vonGal. "It is eclectic but not confused."

Despite the eclecticism, there is a very strong point of view: Plants are used in large numbers appropriate to the size of the estate. In the hosta garden, there are hundreds of hostas; daisies drift in the fields like snow. The only place for fussiness is in the rose garden.

The land has been tamed, one section at a time: The wetlands became a wild garden, a refined, enhanced version of the original, with a walk laid by Bye and Meltzer. About 90 percent of the plants are from Eastern Long Island, many of them native to the property. Meltzer dug up goldenrod, swamp mallow, and butterfly weed in one spot and transplanted them in another, then overseeded the land with Queen Anne's lace. Now the section is mature and only needs one cutting a year.

Even the herb garden, which bridges the space between the parking area and the tennis court, is idealized and planted not so much for kitchen

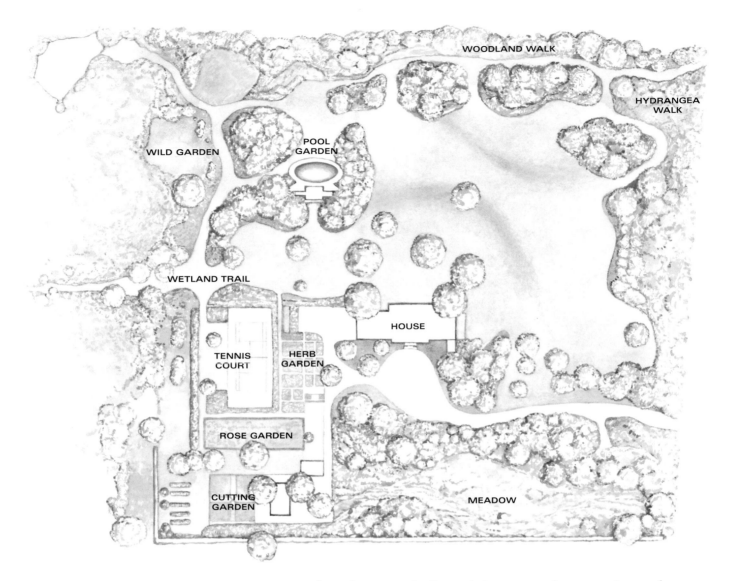

HYDRANGEA
WALK

WILD GARDEN

POOL
GARDEN

WETLAND TRAIL

HOUSE

TENNIS
COURT

HERB
GARDEN

ROSE GARDEN

MEADOW

CUTTING
GARDEN

In May, pink petals from an old Kwansan cherry trace a shadow on the grass at the head of the woodland trail (opposite). A bench, just beyond a curve of the hosta-lined walk, is a secluded spot to stop before heading deeper into the stand of trees.

use as for color—purple. Beyond the rose garden, a cutting garden supplies the main house with summer flowers. "Edwina gave it structure by dividing it into four very formal squares," Meltzer said, "so that I can plant just about anything." Just about anything, in Meltzer terms, means almost 100 different perennials and annuals.

The energetic gardener's latest "event" is a large parcel of land Meltzer bought and saved from subdivision. "We will have mostly grasses with a sequence of wildflowers and local plants—something like what you once would have seen in Hempstead Plain, in the middle of Nassau County, before there was anything built," he said, enthusiasm underscoring his words. Limited to indigenous species, many of which grow wild on the rolling hills of the nearby Shinnecock Golf Club, this will be his tribute to the natural landscape of Long Island. Meltzer—Long Island born and bred—has come home.

A 1,000-foot allée of arborvitae and ornamental rhubarb leading to an iris-fringed lake is typical of the breathtaking scale of Les Quatre Vents (opposite). A Lutyens-inspired arch frames the distant Laurentians. Outside the living room a reflecting pool mirrors two 60-year-old Swiss mountain pines (dwarfed, Frank Cabot says, by neglect) and dianthus pushes through the terrace (above). Beyond, the tapis vert is bracketed by the rose and white gardens.

majestic vision

Ask Frank Cabot about the arch at the end of an allée of arborvitae at Les Quatre Vents, his hilltop garden overlooking the St. Lawrence River northeast of Quebec City, and he will tell you that it was modeled after a design by Sir Edwin Lutyens. "It was for the Royal Mogul Garden in the Viceroy's Palace in New Delhi," he explains. "Except here we substituted arborvitae for banyan trees."

Such a precise response is typical of the septuagenarian patrician, whose passions for history and gardening led him and his wife, Anne, to establish the Garden Conservancy, a group that helps save America's great gardens.

For the past two decades, these twin passions plus a fascination with various architectural responses to gardens throughout the world have also led the Cabots to shape a series of wild and formal gardens, lush woodlands, and hedged outdoor rooms at their 20-acre estate at La Malbaie, populating the spaces with rare plants and linking them to the surrounding landscape with skill and grace.

Frank inherited Les Quatre Vents—once part of a land grant from Louis XIV—in 1965. The garden had been laid out in the 1930s, with axes radiating down and out from the house. Since he started restoring and refining the garden in the late 1970s, it has extended, as he says, "like an ink stain across the land." There are now some eight garden rooms. Sometimes, the estate's soil and cool maritime climate are willing partners in Cabot's magnificent designs: Russell Hybrid lupines, escapees from a formal bed, have taken over a meadow to form an Impressionist masterpiece.

Other sections of the garden required more work: To mimic the mists of a Himalayan cloud forest, a network of timed sprinklers was installed on the steep banks of a deep ravine where streams of Chinese rhubarb ('Atrosanguineum'), ostrich ferns, and heartleaf bergenia grow.

The first section Frank Cabot restored was the Sackville-West–inspired white garden (above), which his mother started in the 1930s. With the help of a Sicilian stone-mason, Cabot rebuilt the wall, using limestone from a nearby quarry. He filled the garden with 300 snowy blooms, many of them alpines, including *Campanula cochleariifolia*. The main perennial borders (opposite) lead from the woodland up steps to the white garden.

Previous page: A meadow
of lupines, straight from an
Impressionist's canvas,
leads to Anne Cabot's hilltop
potager—six large beds
of fruits, vegetables, and
flowers for cutting—guarded
by a pair of scarecrows.
A pool (opposite) mirrors
what Cabot considers one
of his most satisfying projects: a *pigeonnier* framed
by raised hedges of little-
leaf lindens. (Here, the eye
is drawn to the Laurentians.)
Inspiration came from a mill
at Bodnant in Wales, and
an 18th-century tower
Cabot admired in a book
on French farms. "Water
is the dynamic element in
the garden," Cabot states.
"The more the better."
Between columns of
arborvitae and ornamental
rhubarb (above), the Water
Course steps down to a
pond; a birch acts as the
slim white focal point.

The rope bridge that spans this 100-foot-wide gorge was inspired by the Cabots' travels to Asia, as was a teahouse. Other structures spring from Cabot's voluminous reading and his imagination. "I came to appreciate design as the most interesting element in a landscape," he commented, "and readily admit I am a flagrant horticultural plagiarist."

Such plagiarism and irrepressible enthusiasm have paid off: "In the beginning, you had a 360-degree view," said Cabot. "Now, it will take you two hours just to walk through the garden. I have tried to make it appeal to all of the senses, so that it provokes emotional discoveries, so that it is a sensuous as well as an aesthetic experience."

"The most interesting gardens," he added, "often have a numinous spirit." Les Quatre Vents, with its grand scale, adventurous use of architecture, and consummate plantsmanship, certainly possesses such spirit.

A stone stairway, fringed with maidenhair ferns and recently planted Canada hemlock ('Cole's Prostrate'), leads from the dovecote to the Japanese pavilion (right). The bamboo railings create strong lines in the naturalistic setting.

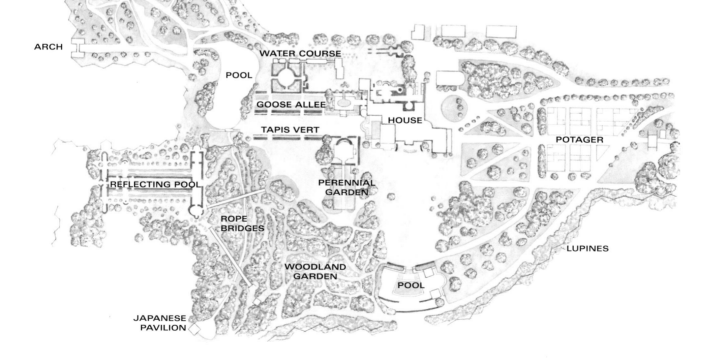

MOON BRIDGE

ARCH

WATER COURSE

POOL

GOOSE ALLEE

HOUSE

TAPIS VERT

POTAGER

REFLECTING POOL

PERENNIAL GARDEN

ROPE BRIDGES

LUPINES

WOODLAND GARDEN

POOL

JAPANESE PAVILION

A dragon moon bridge (above), a copy of a 15th-century one in Guilan, China, makes its serpentine way over a ravine. The original has only one arch, but topography at Les Quatre Vents dictated a second. Nearby, in the Japanese section of the garden, a stone walk leads to a pavilion (left) sited for contemplation while viewing the Laurentians.

the garden
deconstructed

entrances

As every gardener of any merit knows, without structure, a garden is little more than a collection of plants—a dictionary with marvelous entries but no plot, no pacing, no greater theme. And, in every clime except the tropics and subtropics, the foliage disappears with the first frost, a sort of temperature-sensitive Websters printed in Magic Ink.

In this section, the garden is deconstructed: Piece by piece, the elements that go into the makeup of the garden—hedges and walls, fences and gates, paths, terraces, water elements, and so on—are examined.

Although there is an inevitable overlap—the entrance garden requires paths and steps to terraces; outdoor rooms are defined by walls, hedges, and fences—the intention is to focus on the essence of each category as revealed through the various solutions of landscape architects, designers, and dedicated gardeners.

The entrance to a garden is like the beginning of a novel: In a few sentences,

Sharon Casdin and designer John Saladino collaborated to transform a plain stretch of yard into a gracious entrance to the Casdins' 1762 New England house. A fence, inspired by an 1850 tintype, encloses a generous lawn punctuated with rectangular beds. Casdin, a flower designer, planted perennials that could have been selected by the original owners: peonies, daylilies, phlox. To make simple stairs connecting the garden to the house, Saladino ordered huge slabs of granite from a local quarry.

Clockwise from top left: In keeping with the comfortable formality of Charlotte Moss' Long Island home, a walk of cut bluestone leisurely steps up to the house through an allée of urns and 'Bradford' pears. In Provence, a heavy wooden door that once shut off the 17th-century monastery from the sins of the world now leads to a weekend retreat. A glimpse of the luxuriant gardens planted by Nancy Goslee Power lures the visitor down narrow stairs covered by a dense canopy of bougainvillea. John Saladino "restored" the Santa Barbara home, lightly sand-blasting the bright white of painted stone to suggest that this is indeed an ancient place. Bringing a bit of Tuscany to Los Angeles, Cheryl Lerner salvaged the gates from an old building, painted them green to match the shutters of her house, and mounted them on new posts. Red poppies, roses, nasturtium, and purple lavender enlarge on the exuberant Mediterranean theme.

the author sets the tone. An entrance, as Christopher Alexander wrote in his book *A Pattern Language*, can sometimes "relate a feeling of a private domain and a world apart."

Sometimes an entrance defines the style of an entire garden, be it classical or modern, cottage or formal: The period is set through the use of plants and hardscape, and the rest of the garden expands upon the theme, rather like the social novels of Trollope or Mahfouz. At other times, the entrance builds expectations only to confound them, as it does at Albert Hadley's Connecticut home. There a diminutive picture-perfect period garden leads to an Italianate Victorian house, but in the back expands and metamorphizes into a water garden, which, in turn, is overlooked by a classic American screened porch.

Depending on the architecture and setting of the house, and the personality of the owner, an entrance garden can instill a sense of calm stateliness or an air of mystery and intrigue. Behind a high wall, a few select plants and a simple fountain can let the visitor know she has entered a retreat for contemplation, set quite apart from the rest of the world. Or, with a low picket fence, a wide gate, and a straightforward path, a garden can open itself to the street in a sense of democratic neighborliness.

Often, multiple entries contribute to the whole. A drive through a forest can be one entrance, a broad path across a slight rise wrapped in groundcover another, a narrow passageway leading off the main path to a less public section of the garden a third. One entrance can be divided into parts, as in Ben Page's garden, where a gate opens off the sidewalk into a "decompression" entry hall, which leads in turn to the main garden.

Regardless of the style of entrance, the implicit promise of welcome should be understood: A place large enough for guests to orient themselves, to savor the garden while waiting to be greeted. As Thomas Church, the eminent California landscape architect, put it so practically: "Nothing justifies making an obstacle course out of the trip from the car to the front door."

A path between the low wall and a hedge of reeds (opposite) links a 20th-century treasure—Case Study House #9, designed by Charles Eames and Eero Saarinen in 1949—and a new, and separate, Cubist-inspired residence designed by architect Barry A. Berkus. The landscape design for the new complex, conceived by the late Emmet L. Wemple and executed by Marc Fisher of Sierra Madre, California, hides worldly sights and sounds while echoing the rectilinear shape of the glass-walled landmark. Lit at night, the entry is glorious.

Mindful that the idea of outdoor living in urban Southern California is often much more pleasant in theory than reality, New Jersey landscape architect Robert Breen created what he calls an "outdoor party room" (above) for a house designed by the late Paul Rudolph. Columns of wisteria twist up and overrun a grid of tension wires to make a canopy over the entrance court. Closed off from the street by walls patterned with espaliered fruit trees, the tiled space quickly converts to this century's equivalent of an outdoor ballroom.

inside out

porches & patios

OUTDOOR LIVING SPACES ARE TRANSITIONS FROM THE ENCLOSURE OF THE home to the openness of our natural surroundings, fulfilling what Thomas Church called "our longing to live in our site." Inside/out spaces—be they descendants of the secluded Spanish patio, formal stone loggias borrowing from Italian design, or a wooden deck 20 feet above the ground amongst the treetops—should fit the style of the house, the garden, and—this is most important—fulfill our expectations of what they will do for us. Are they to protect us from attacking hordes of blood-sucking insects? Bring on the screened porch, that most delightful architectural ode to summer evenings, a spot to listen to the call of whippoorwills, to smell and hear the rain as it strikes the earth just outside. Or is it to provide a view worthy of a hawk's aerie? Let us have a terrace *à la* Church, boldly jutting into the void of some canyon.

There are many options, too many perhaps for a decision to be made before settling into the garden and realizing what type of outdoor space is really needed. Landscape architect Ben Page and his wife, who love to entertain in their small garden in Nashville, after a false start decided to set the terrace at a distance from the town house, requiring a quick walk through the vegetable garden parterre. He paved the terrace in local stone and made sure it was wide enough that guests would not unwillingly fall into the fountain pool (an activity eagerly engaged in by his daughter and her friends).

In the Berkeley hills overlooking San Francisco Bay, the home of architects Marcy Wong and Donn Logan opens to a garden atrium designed by Ron Lutsko (opposite). Just off the kitchen, wooden slats lightly shade a dining area perched atop a series of tiny terraces, planted with fleabane (*Erigeron*), blue oat grass (*Helictotrichon*), and loropetalum, and walled in the same rough-textured cement block used in the house. The screened porch— that time-honored American summer institution—is idealized by designer Robert Currie (above), who specified antique wicker furniture and white cushions, accented with antique linens from the owner's collection.

For a one-terrace-only garden, it is wise—if possible—to have part of the space in shade and part in sun. Larger gardens allow for multiple terraces, one warmed by the early morning sun for breakfast, one sheltered from night winds for dinner, still another more remote and secluded for privacy. In the same breath, one must repeat the admonition of French gardener Albert Maumone: "If you are discreet, you will realize that one terrace, well kept up, is much more valuable than several left in disrepair." Portable chairs and a flat piece of land, a blanket and umbrella are the minimalist's instant terrace.

Whatever style of outdoor room is selected, fragrant plants are welcome additions, although the degree and type of fragrance is a highly individual, even controversial, one. For Reginald Farrer, the botanist/ plant-hunter/dedicated gardener, no scent could be too excessive: "People may swoon all round me from Jasmine or Gardenia: at each whiff I grow stronger, and my thoughts clearer, and hopes higher. . . ." His friend A.E. Bowles, on the other hand, had a nose so discerning that a "dinner table decorated heavily with sweet peas spoils my dinner, as I taste Sweet Peas with every course . . . whilst they ruin the bouquet of good wine." *Chacun a son goût.*

"A porch is a wonderful mid-way space," according to interior designer David Easton, "sheltered but still outdoors." He has two mid-way spaces jutting at right angles from each end of his home (above). The idea for rose trellises on the roof was taken from a restaurant in Nantucket; a fireplace—to take the chill off of spring and autumn evenings—was inspired by one at a club in Northeast Harbor, Maine.

A classic open-air porch, called a "piazza" on the 1894 plans, sweeps around a corner of the house owned by Peter Ermacora and Evan G. Hughes (opposite), two design consultants who use antiques as centerpieces to their designs. Only a low fieldstone wall and a hedge of euonymus separates the garden from the comfortable sitting area.

All that is needed in an open-air sitting room, like the one at the Hollywood home of furniture designers Steven Charlton and Jeffrey Goodman (opposite above), are a lounger, walls draped in old vines of creeping fig and bougainvillea, and two clumps of newly planted tall grasses. With a long stretch of canvas-covered cushions and a few chairs, Anne-Marie de Ganay transformed a corner of her dining terrace into a spot to enjoy aperitifs (opposite below). Craving privacy for their outdoor dining room in a Los Angeles housing complex, the decorator/architect team Kate and Odom Stamps trained passion-flower vines over a metal frame typically used to support more traditional coverings (above right). In England, an umbrella and a lone tree provide sufficient shade on Nancy Lancaster's tastefully simple terrace (below right).

With the right trees, who
needs architecture? At the
family's weekend retreat,
the sons of architects Mary
Griffin and William Turnbull
bathe al fresco (above). With
49 acres of vineyards, all
that is needed is an old claw-
foot tub, a sheltering valley
oak, a few pots with scented flowers—and some soap.

At the back of Hitch Lyman's
Greek Revival home outside
of Ithaca, New York, clipped
linden trees—what the garden designer and painter
calls "a souvenir of the Plaka
in Athens"—shade the ter-
race (right). A scented
carpet of creeping thyme
and silver tansy surges
down stone steps to the
lawn.

the skeleton
walls & hedges

"EVERY GARDEN, LARGE OR SMALL, OUGHT TO BE PLANNED FROM THE OUTSET, getting its bones, its skeleton, into the shape that it will preserve all through the year even after the flowers have faded and died away." Thus wrote Victoria Sackville-West, England's justly renowned literary gardener. She was speaking about the massing of colors, but the thought can be applied to the more permanent skeleton of the garden—the hedges and walls—and the paths that are its lifeblood. Without this architecture, as so many writers have said, a garden is little more than a collection of plants. Walls and hedges not only give structure, but provide a stage set for flowers, a protective barrier against harsh winds.

In classical times, walls enclosed the garden, which became an extra room. In the Middle Ages, the *hortus conclusus* was a walled retreat tucked away from the dark world. Renaissance gardens of the 17th century were divided into compartments, with varying themes; after William Kent, the 18th-century English

Hedges become verdant walls in the simple, refined court of a Hancock Park, California, residence. New Jersey landscape architects Zion and Breen limited the types of plants used, specifying a double row of Italian cypress to screen out the neighbors, and a diamond grid of espaliered fruit trees to decorate a cement wall. The space is a study in textures and light. The serene green palette is broken only when the lavender-colored wisteria is in flower.

designer of Stowe, "leaped the fence" and opened up the "landskip," walls were relegated to enclosing the functional parts of gardens. By the end of the 19th century, however, following the lead of William Robinson and Gertrude Jekyll, walls of masonry and clipped hedges were again used for the ornamental garden, creating "rooms" to be furnished with flowers.

Retaining walls, as Thomas Church so plainly put it, should be used "when the bulldozer leaves the property looking as if it had been hit by a blockbuster." As a bonus, these walls offer a setting for micro-gardens: small plants that would otherwise be lost in a large landscape. These include alpines for those who like plants that need cherishing. Other people, who, in the words of Christopher Lloyd, "just like a jolly assemblage

After a trip to England and visits to Sissinghurst and Great Dixter, George Schoellkopf returned to his 18th-century Connecticut home, his head "filled with visions of old brick walls smothered in climbing roses." Realizing such plans "might be just a bit too grand for the house," he placed the main garden, with its eight-foot walls, well to the side of the house, so that there would be no vista on a central axis.

that will take care of itself," would be wise to follow his suggestions in *The Adventurous Gardener*. Walls typically match the house: a brick wall works well with brick, fieldstone with Yankee clapboard.

Hedges have the advantage over masonry in that they are, at the outset, less expensive, and will block wind without creating their own wind currents. Formally cut, or natural and billowing, they not only define the boundaries of the garden, they introduce the space: Hedges can smell sweet and provide movement, texture, and even sound (their own, as well as the calls of birds that love hiding and nesting in them). And while hedges do require maintenance, depending on the type and the style of trimming, it need not be burdensome.

When planning a hedge, the garden as a whole must be considered: A tall hedge will cut off the sight of a parking lot—and also any borrowed view of distant mountains, a church steeple, a towering old chestnut tree. A row of barbed *Rosa rugosa* can serve as a barrier to a steep drop; ground-hugging hedges of catnip, lavender, and rosemary can define and fringe a path.

If hedges are meant to be as substantial as a brick wall, blocking all

In a small Atlanta garden, an irregular dry stone wall separates the pool from a woodland known as the Secret Garden (opposite). In the more formal garden of the respected Belgian designer Jacques Wirtz (above), low, geometrically shaped hedges lead to the narrow slit in a crenelated hedge.

views at all times, they should be year-round green walls of boxwood, yew, holly, arborvitae, or cypress. This evergreen architecture weatherproofs a garden even in the bleakest of months. On the other hand, if a hedge is needed only for a season, as are those marching the perimeters around the grand summer estates of the Hamptons on Long Island, deciduous shrubs will suffice.

Although hedges tend to be of one type of bush, a delightful tapestry effect can be achieved by using more than one cultivar (a particularly glorious example of this resides at Hidcote). The English hedgerow, a mixture of species that usually includes dogwood, wild cherry, and hawthorn, can be customized for one's own garden with an assortment of flowering bushes—hydrangeas, mock orange, lilac—to create an informal windscreen that is both redolent and colorful.

In Europe there is a long
tradition of using hedges to
form the shape of a garden.
In Mark Rudkin's garden
southwest of Paris (left
above and below), entrances
off the central corridor of
variegated hornbeam lead to
rooms that are still attractive
at season's end. Opposite,
clockwise from above left:
The sculpted boxwoods in
Jacques Wirtz's garden are
mesmerizing in all seasons.
David Hicks carefully planned
the structure of his
Oxfordshire garden before a
spade was lifted. In a vernal
trompe l'oeil, twin rows of
hornbeam are pruned to
resemble pleached trees; a
path mown through the tall
grass runs through a pasture
beyond. In a town garden
designed by the grande
dame of Dutch landscape
design, Mien Ruys, a path of
square paving stones shadows the rectangle carved
into a high hornbeam wall
that separates the garden
from the street. A window in
a hedge of *Carpinus betulus*
allows a tantalizing peek into
the next section of her garden in Dedemsvaart; the
counterpoint of flowing,
flowering bushes is typical
of her designs, which have
been likened to an
Impressionist painting super-
imposed over a Piet
Mondrian canvas.

fences & gates

Before entering Chotsie Blank's rose and herb garden, where bearded irises and chives thrive in raised rectangular beds, visitors must pass through a weathered gate, crowned with a trellis of 'Zephirine Drouhin' roses. "Some of the English roses will keep growing through the summer here in Napa Valley, but the bloom is smaller and the color often fades in the heat," said Roger Warner, the landscape designer who worked with Blank on the layout of the formal garden.

SINCE THE EUROPEANS SETTLED IN THE NEW WORLD, FENCES AND GATES HAVE been part of the American landscape. The Dutch erected wooden barriers, delineating civilization and wilderness: Anyone sent beyond the pale was considered lost to society.

Today, the fence can do the reverse: delineate one's private wilderness from the rest of civilization. Fences are the nation's favorite way to establish boundaries, undoubtedly because they are cheaper (at least initially) than walls, and take less time to stake a claim than hedges.

Deer fences can save hedges and trees from hungry herds; the chain link is the conventional choice to secure pools, catch stray tennis balls, and, with luck, discourage wandering dogs. Admittedly the Plain Jane of the family, the chain link can be dressed up and even made pretty if clothed in roses or vines. Wire fences have traditionally been used on farm land to establish cheap barriers between livestock and public roads. Draped in wild bittersweet and honeysuckle these simple cross-country wanderers have their own unselfconscious charm. Because of their malleable nature, they can be fashioned into various shapes: In one Long Island garden, a wire fence was scalloped to mimic the curves of a neighboring brick wall.

Fences and gates can also be used as a transition, a visual cue that one is leaving one part of the garden and entering another. Sometimes there is good cause for these barriers. It is common to enclose vegetable plots with fences (which, if backed with wire mesh dug into the ground, can help dissuade furry intruders). But other times, it is more psychological: A heavy wooden door permanently ajar still imparts the sense of something hidden, perhaps secret. In Japan, a "gate" as simple as a segment of bamboo on foot-high posts can be an indicator of a path closed.

A fence and gate should never dominate a garden, but should compliment the house and the surrounding neighborhood: If a fence is to be used

as fronting for a Federal house, some type of picket is almost a foregone conclusion, though what style of picket may depend on the state, the neighborhood, and of course, personal taste. Even something as ordinary as the split-rail fence, that quicksilver delineator that runs like basting stitches across the countryside, has its regional variations, from New England to Pennsylvania, Virginia, Colorado, and Wyoming.

Details such as the style of pales, posts, and piers, as well as the finials, caps, urns, and balls that crown them, can be relatively inexpensive ways to establish a garden's character, as can the choice of the color of paint, or the lack of it.

A solid fence is a good way to insure privacy. Landscape architect Raymond Jungles used inexpensive galvanized metal sheet and chain-link fences to screen off his corner garden from the street, then painted them black and planted them with vines to make the homely barriers "disappear." If there is no need for a physical boundary, a mostly open fence will suggest a boundary without being an actual barrier. Such fences allow not only wind, but light to enter—an important part of the drama of the garden.

In the grand tradition of Adirondack Camps (above), architect Peter Bohlin set this scene of intentional rusticity, carefully specifying the fence's every intersection of branches, and positioning each piece of obstructing granite. A low split-rail fence visually connects the stone barn to the yard leading up to the 1820s Pennsylvania farmhouse (opposite). It also warns potential stragglers of the steep drop from an old stone wall, while the attached chicken wire dissuades barnyard strays from making a meal of the lawn.

Fences often serve as a visual break, a friendly border between a village yard and a close-by sidewalk, or a manicured little plot and a field gone wild. A low white picket fence (opposite above), in keeping with the 18th-century house nearby, separates a lush flower garden from a meadow that stretches to Long Island Sound. The hand-turned finials on Hannah Wister's colonial-style fence (opposite bottom) are copies of the cornice of her 18th-century house in New Jersey. The fence serves both as a deterrent to deer and a demarcation between the geometrical vegetable and flower garden and the rest of the grounds. The utilitarian need not be mundane (above right). At Old River Gardens near Clay, Texas, a barbed-wire fence entwined with a muscadine grapevine cuts through a field of Indian paintbrush. At a Bucks County, Pennsylvania, farm, a rustic fence and arbor separates the garden from the lawn leading to the 1830s farmhouse, stopping deer but allowing breezes to pass unabated (below right). Willis Watts built the fence from young cedars and landscape designer John Carloftis fashioned a curved bench out of saplings.

David Hicks, one of England's most distinguished interior designers, exerted his considerable talents outside in the garden attached to his 150-year-old house in Oxfordshire (above left). Nodding to the architecture of his home, he designed Gothic-style gates, one of which leads to the green-house area. On the other side of the Atlantic in Nashville (below left), an ironwork panel in a heavy wooden door gives a glimpse of a walled city garden. Ben Page lightened the sedate mood with a snail making its way up the gate. A rustic gate marks the entrance to Ryan Gainey's Atlanta garden (opposite), where a hand-painted tile of the First Couple gives a hint of what to expect in this personal Eden. Black-eyed Susans wait outside, while inside 10-foot-high sunflowers explode into golden stars. Beyond the gate, stepping stones, embedded in gravel, lead to parterres overflowing with lettuces, peas, beans, red-veined Swiss chard, and other earthly delights.

paths & steps

IN *THE EDUCATION OF A GARDENER*, RUSSELL PAGE WROTE: "PATHS ARE all-important. Before I begin to elaborate my composition, I like to establish . . . the lines of communication between house and garden."

Paths not only lead us from point A to point B (although that is a primary concern). They are "the skeleton of the garden," as the English gardener and writer Rosemary Verey told Gordon Hayard in his comprehensive book, *Garden Paths*: "They frame beds into manageable sizes and divide the garden into different areas, leading you on from one section to the next, through gates, under archways, round corners, and along vistas." A good path is an irrestitible invitation.

Paths let us know the garden in physical as well as psychological ways: A grand 20-foot-wide gravel axial path by Le Nôtre compelled everyone travelling it to recognize the power of the Sun King. The very same gravel forming a narrow "bachelor" path encourages a sense of introspection. Even in the most suburban gardens, there are different paths for different purposes: the entrance path, the path to the garage (typically evenly surfaced, straight or slightly curved—the path of least resistance), a path to a shaded bench, the path through a wood. In small gardens, the use of one or two types of paving can unify the garden and connect it to the house, as in the case of Nancy Goslee Power's use of granite flagstones and crushed stone for interior designer Ann James' modest Los Angeles garden. On the other hand, varying the types of paving material can lend a sense of multiplicity to a garden, when done with finesse. When landscape designer Roger Warner changed the gravel path to brick in Chotsie Blank's herb garden in Napa Valley, he alternated not only the color, but the texture, pattern, and under-foot feel of the path. A change in a path at a gate or under an archway is a visual, sensory, and audible cue that the stroller is entering another space.

Clockwise from top left: A circle of square-cut granite blocks from a local quarry radiates out to create a stairway as pleasing to the eyes as it is to the feet in Frank Cabot's Canadian garden; tufts of alpines soften the strict geometry. In Connecticut, designer John Funt laid Belgian paving blocks on a sunny slope outside his dining room and planted both woolly and common thyme. "Thyme is perfect for dry, hot conditions," Funt said. "And it is nice to walk out and smell crushed thyme underfoot." In moist, shady areas, a carpet of moss can withstand light traffic, as illustrated by steps designed by the late landscape architect Fletcher Steele. For a change of pace, Jacques Wirtz of Belgium intersected a gravel path with herringbone brick that ends, abruptly, surprisingly, at a neoclassical bust resting in a hedge's verdant niche.

Paths reflect not only their use, but their environment. At designer Renny Reynolds' farm in Bucks County, Pennsylvania (top left), an informal woodchip path slips into the woods, away from a rustic bridge fashioned of branches cut from a fallen tree. The Japanese have long used irregularly spaced stepping stones to speed or slow a stroller's pace, subtly guiding him to look, see, smell, experience the unfolding journey (below left). Such techniques have been imported to this country, sometimes with great success, as evidenced by a path in the John P. Humes Japanese Stroll Garden in Mill Neck, New York. Broad grass paths, cut by a single swing of a mower, or planted in a woodland, as in Robert Meltzer's Southampton, New York, garden (opposite above), are emblematic of carefree summer days—pastoral invitations for a leisurely stroll. Closer to a house, narrower paved walks suggest a more civilized setting. Erica Shank and Bill Shank laid a gently curving brick and bluestone path along the front of this house on Long Island (opposite below). Weeping grasses and low, spreading creepers lightly play against the formal pattern.

The course of a path influences the way in which we see and experience a garden: It gives us a sense of the unity of the space and builds our expectations. The Japanese have long been masters of directing the stroller's attention via a path, urging one to walk fast (wide path, even stones), slow (flat, unevenly spaced stones), to stop and look down (uneven, rounded stones; a narrow, irregular boardwalk). "The path," as Robert Dash, painter and garden designer has said, "is how the garden is known."

There are many types of paving materials, each with its own special traits. The smell and the feel of grass underfoot (especially when one is barefoot) is the essence of summer. "Grass," wrote Russell Page, "is one of the most sumptuous and extravagant materials for a wide path." However, Christopher Lloyd is quite clear about the use of such an extravagance: it should not be made "if traffic is so heavy as to wear it to mud." The baby of all paths, the grass path is not for the low-maintenance garden: It is in constant need of nurturing (watering, cutting, feeding, reseeding).

Cut stone is the most formal paving. Highly geometric, it is best for straight or slightly curved walks; its smooth surface makes it easy to shovel in snow, and admirably useful when sure footing is required. In selecting stone, typically it is wisest to use a stone indigenous to the region, although the rule can be broken. Cut stone as well as other stone paths offer an excellent place for small plants to take residence between the pavers.

Fieldstone walks, what Gordon Hayward calls "stone carpets," are by definition more informal and tend to give a garden a natural feeling, because of the randomness of their size and color. These paths can easily follow the contour of the land and "dissolve" into the landscape.

Brick walkways tend to be warm, inviting, less formal than cut stones, and more colorful and declarative than fieldstone. Depending on the type of bricks and the way in which they are set (there are literally dozens of patterns), a brick path can bring to mind an English country garden, an Italian courtyard, or American Colonial or even Modern styles. Because of their diminutive, regular shape, bricks can be used to create a variety of shaped paths: straight, zig-zag, curving, circular. They are also useful in edging. Handmade bricks or recycled old bricks lend character to a pathway, and are superior to many newer bricks. Placed on their edge, bricks can make very narrow paths through meadows or orchards, and

Inspired by a visit to Villa Gamberaia, Italy, Ben and Libby Page painstakingly laid a mosaic of black, white, and pink river stones in the "entry hall" to their small city garden. "It's just like putting a fabulous rug in the vestibule," Ben said. Signifying a change of scene, a brick walk continues on through a wall of arborvitae into the main garden.

suggest a slim, visual line that pulls the stroller through an otherwise open landscape. Paving stones can be used like brick, but lend a more citified, sophisticated air to a walkway.

Concrete is the stuff for a durable, no-maintenance walkway. In the right hands, concrete can be laid to make not only an inexpensive, fluid path but also one that is quite beautiful and imaginative. The late Thomas Church used it to fine advantage at his own home in San Francisco, its gray tone and rough texture complement the gray wooden house, the stairs, and the dark green plants around the entrance. Concrete embedded with aggregate can echo the architecture of the house (a frequent and laudable practice by Western landscape architects like Ron Lutsko and Bill Hays), while precast concrete pavers have been used to fine effect as utilitarian and highly patterned paths by such illustrious gardeners as England's Rosemary Verey and Georgia's Ryan Gainey.

Wood boardwalks immediately bring to mind water: the ocean beach, a lakeside dock, or a path to a stream or marsh. Although painted wood steps can be used as an entrance to a formal home, wood tends to work best in informal, natural settings. Wood can also be used in conjunction with other materials, something as hard as pea gravel or as soft as moss or thyme, creating variegated steps that slow one's progress and compell one to take in the surrounding scenery and scents.

Gravel, crushed stone, and pea stone are flexible materials extremely useful for paths that must bend and buckle. They come in a variety of colors and textures (as well as sounds), but, as is the case with other paving, it is usually best to stick with local sources, so that the color will blend with the soil (white pea stone, for instance, works well for paths on sandy, Long Island gardens while decayed granite looks better in Texas).

Pine needles, bark, mulch, and trodden dirt (the simplest of all paths) are the way we get to know forests and wood gardens. Moss, a velvety, silent living cousin of these more robust materials, requires attention and maintenance, but its serenity can be appreciated in more places than a Zen garden.

At Richard Martin's home in a canyon above Los Angeles, waves of woolly and creeping thyme ripple over shallow treads that lead from the Mediterranean garden up to the olive grove (above right). The architect and landscape designer Nancy Goslee Power planned the garden on the ground, tramping around the site, laying out paths with white gypsum powder. Architect Byron Bell wrapped a retreat in rural New York with wood decking, and then extended a boardwalk to the lake front, cascading the stairs down the grassy hill (below right). The stairway allows the homeowners to take advantage of a 30-mile view to Connecticut and still have access to a man-made pond.

allées, pergolas & arches

Some of the most spectacular scenes in the horticultural theater we call a garden are achieved with little more than a few simple metal frames and some thoughtful planting: Think of rose-covered arches leading to the front door at Monet's pink farmhouse in Giverny and you'll understand immediately. Just as the stage designer uses frames, screens, and light to create the illusion of space and place, so the gardener suggests quite substantial architecture with the most basic structures—the arch; its multiple, the tunnel or gallery; and the slightly more complex structures of arbors and pergolas.

An arch can signify an entrance, the beginning of a path. It frames a still-life, and yet beckons the visitor to walk on, to enter the scene. Planted with sweet-scented climbers—roses, jasmine, honeysuckle, wisteria—it immediately treats the visitor to more than the visual delights of the garden.

A tunnel—a series of metal or lath arches that disappears in the vines it supports—heightens the sense of suspense, encompassing the stroller, directing his progress and shaping his vision in an emphatic way no other garden element can. Inside the green gallery, the rest of the world disappears—a highly felicitous device, particularly if a nearby part of the world is unattractive or, as in the case of some 18th-century palace gardens, so beautiful as to be too distracting.

A less didactic version of the tunnel, the arbor rises free-standing in the garden, a vertical point of interest in a predominantly horizontal landscape. Sometimes the arbor stands unadorned, marking boundaries, tracking the progress of a path. Other times it is as much vegetation as man-made structure, providing support for climbing vines, giving shade to those who would enjoy it. The pergola, its less adventuresome sibling, attaches itself to the house—a verdant, open-air room.

For a few weeks every spring, azaleas and painted locust posts create a fiery allée in the green piney woods surrounding the intriguing LongHouse Reserve in East Hampton, Long Island. Jack Lenor Larsen, the inspired creator of these grounds, is a master of deception: The "massive" water urn is, in fact, only a few feet high. The plants and posts are graduated in size, and the path narrows as it would on an artist's canvas to show perspective. (Not content to play his trick once a year, Larsen plants banners—once again successively smaller—in the summer months.)

Somewhere in between these built structures and the simple path is the allée or avenue, a formal corridor open to the sky and flanked quite often by two columns of trees standing at attention, evenly spaced and tall. Cypress are frequent recruits, but bushes, statues, pots, posts, and even flags can be enlisted, all marching toward some vista—whimsical or sublime—the gardener is determined you will see. Whatever is used, the linear perspective gives an impression of distance, particularly useful in small gardens.

While such grand garden flourishes can require legions of stone masons, gardeners and (consequently) a Swiss bank account, one needn't use Carrara marble for the columns and wrought iron for the arches. Arbors can be made of concrete rubble covered with stucco, steel or plastic pipes painted dark green, wooden posts or black locust cleared from an overgrown field. Nor need these airy bits of architecture always be paired with roses: Grapevines do well in sunny climes, as do clematis and jasmine; for the impatient, climbing squash vines or morning glories will suffice. For those expecting a long run, the choices of actors are wide: apple, pear, hornbeam. But do not be fooled: As strong and willful a vine as wisteria will need strong support.

Architect Edward Knowles designed an arbor for this Nantucket garden (above). A simplified adaptation of an arbor at Dumbarton Oaks, the structure frames one side of a sunken croquet court, flanked by profuse beds of perennials. A lattice pavilion and arbor neatly echo the bronzes and golds of *Sambucus racemosa* 'Plumosa Aurea', ornamental rhubarb, and other rare plants at Heronswood Nursery in Kingston, Washington (opposite).

At Cheryl K. Lerner's home in Los Angeles, the garden designer turned a patio into an outdoor living room (opposite), where an old hybrid tea rose, 'Lady Forteviot', rambles over a pergola. Following a Mediterranean theme, Lerner had the concrete pavers dyed to match the terra-cotta pots, which hold a moveable garden of plants from southern Europe. In France's first formal rose garden, Roseriaie de L'Hay-les-Roses, planted in 1893, two paths veer off to shape a heavenly stereoscopic vision of rose-covered tunnels, with passionate-hued 'Dorothy Perkins' rose leading to pale pink 'New Dawn' and darker 'Excelsa' (above right). Lynden Miller was a painter before she became a garden designer. Her "artist's eye" is evident in the restoration of Central Park's Conservatory Garden, as well as her own garden in Connecticut (below right), where a field of Queen Anne's lace surrounds a forget-me-not blue arbor and bench.

water

Throughout history, water features have been intimately associated with gardens: Twin waterways divided the ancient Persian courtyard gardens into quarters, symbolizing the geography of the universe. So important was water to the Japanese garden that, in its absence, Zen masters designed dry waterfalls: boulders, rocks, pebbles, sand, and moss that, through their placement and apparent motion, gave the impression of a natural cascade. In the West, the use of water in the formal garden reached its zenith in the gardens of Renaissance Italy, where water flowed in a variety of guises—springs, spouts, parterres, jets, runnels, rills, cascades, channels (some imitating coats of arms). Throughout the mid-18th century, English landscape gardeners improved on natural bodies of water, sculpting serpentine lakes and ponds and connecting them with cascades and streams.

Today, few gardeners have the space, let alone the resources to employ such grand waterworks. Still, even in the most modest garden, water can expand the feeling of space, acting as a magnet to light, introducing movement and sound. Water opens a whole new realm of planting possibilities, not only aquatics—plants that can grow in airless soil—but also boggy plants—moisture-loving primrose and iris—plants that look as if they love water. One of the simplest, least work-intensive ways to bring water into the garden is the fountain—ranging from urns to stones in geometric shapes like the one in Mien Ruys' Wild Garden.

Clockwise from top left: At the center of a square grass space defined by a low brick wall and a bluestone path, the circular pool, encompassed by more bluestone, sits framed by a square of English ivy. Ten feet in diameter, the pool reflects Albert Hadley's dictum: "A large object makes a small room appear bigger." A stream bed in Jean Pope's New Jersey garden offers Japanese primrose, cinnamon fern, and white azaleas a shady haven. David Hicks' black pool defines the width of an axial mown path that cuts through hornbeams and pasture, past a copse to the vanishing point. Encircled with Canadian hemlock, its irregular paving stones half hidden in moss, this fountain garden is not in Italy but New York, product of the efforts of painter/garden designer Hitch Lyman and owner Laura Fisher.

Before embarking on the rough seas of more extensive water gardening one should be forewarned. That most prickly of British garden writers, Reginald Farrer, was typically outspoken on the subject: "Advice to those about to build a Water garden—DON'T. Not that the water-garden is not a joy and a glory; but it is cruelly hard to keep in order and control unless you are master of millions. . . . Water, like fire, is a good servant, perhaps, but is painfully liable to develop into a master." Even the democratic, supportive Thomas Church, whose designs of pools in California are masterpieces of the genre, was blunt: "The garden pool means hard work. It must be kept clean and well-groomed."

The nature of a garden site will determine the suitability of the type of water garden. Water lilies and most other aquatics, for instance, require direct sunlight to bloom—half a day at least. But gardeners blessed with such a site must realize that algae, too, thrive in sunlight.

In a formal garden, geometric shapes of canals, rills, and pools can promote the garden's design, mirroring clipped hedges, bringing in the light of the sky, giving an illusion of space.

A natural running stream "is one of the very best settings for beautiful

Two water gardens in Southern California designed by Nancy Goslee Power reflect the various moods that can be achieved through the use of vegetation, paving, and ornamentation. In the bright garden of Ann James (above), water trickles from a lazy frog in a trough surrounded with local sand-colored flagstone and gravel paths. In a shady coastal garden (opposite), a more formal, romantic mood prevails, where splashes of pink and blue blossoms overflow into a shady lily pond.

plants," said Gertrude Jekyll, "especially if it flows fast over a shallow pebbly bed, with natural or artificial banks near the water-level." She added that "a wise restraint should be observed about the numbers of different plants that are to be seen at a glance." Those fortunate enough to have a stream should follow her advice.

And while it helps to have a ground source of water on the property, rainfall can be put to very good use, as illustrated by the garden of James David and Gary Peese in Austin, Texas. Here, water is stored in a cistern and then allowed to run, on special occasions, through the garden along a series of water channels, ponds, and basins that lead to a dry creek.

It is no secret to anyone who has seen the raised carp pool at Hidcote (originally designed as a family swimming pool) that a pool need not be a giant blue kidney bean. By its very size, a pool is a dominant design element in the garden's composition and, with thoughtful design, a sympathetic one, as the pools in this section suggest.

In Nashville, clipped box parterres turn a swimming pool into a reflecting pool reminiscent of those gracing 17th-century French gardens (above). John Saladino borrowed from the faded grandeur of Spanish missions at this California estate (left), where a wide stairway marches to the pool. The white-stone walls were sandblasted to give a quick patina. In San Miguel de Allende (opposite), stone lions—reminiscent of earlier Mexican statuary—feed the pool and luxuriant plants grow in profusion, a fancifully reimagined Yucatan jungle.

summer houses &
other structures

IN THE DAYS OF MARIE ANTOINETTE, SIMPLE COTTAGES SPROUTED UP AS decorations in royal gardens: "It shows us a dwelling where happiness may reside unsupported by wealth—as it shows us a resource where we may still continue to enjoy peace," she announced, "though we should be deprived of all the favours of fortune."

The lady had a particular penchant for delusion, but—in the case of summer houses, at least—it is a delusion that many gardeners share. Gazebos, follies, moon-viewing pavilions, tea houses—every country with a history of gardening has had its own style, and frequently has borrowed those of others'. Stowe, the estate of Lord Cobham where master gardeners William Kent and Capability Brown executed their magic, had over two dozen such structures, among them the temple of Modern Virtue, which included a headless statue of Cobham's chief political enemy, Walpole.

Heirs to these flights of architectural fantasy frequently appear in modern gardens, admittedly less grandiose or acidly droll, special places set quite apart from the hurly-burly of mundane life. No temporal distractions will be found in such a spot, no furniture save a bench or a few seats, a table perhaps. Covered roof is optional.

Set apart from time and place, summer houses are structures more of the imagination than the quotidian. Architects Mary Griffin and William Turnbull Jr. built a redwood chapel for their wedding (the two crosses are soldered plumbing pipes). Perched up the hill from their weekend retreat, the gazebo is an out-of-the-way destination, a place for meditation. Entwined with star jasmine and wisteria, the airy structure provides only shade (even the roof is made of open slats)—and the land's most spectacular view of the vineyard.

A pavilion by Dale Booher
and Lisa Stamm of Shelter
Island, New York, is redolent
of Asian mystery, a Kubla
Khan retreat washed by the
sound of a fountain and bells
(opposite). A terrace off
Hitch Lyman's Greek Revival
house overlooks his modern-
day Doric temple (above), a
confabulation of second-hand
19th-century columns and
arched trolley doors—housing
a lawn mower.

Stylistically the summer house can be a distant, diminutive cousin of the main house with prominent familial traits or, if hidden away, the house of one's dreams. A focal point in the garden, the summer house is also a place from which to survey the grounds from a very particular and privileged point of view, and—when covered with a roof—it is a place to enjoy the pleasures of the garden in the rain.

The summer house is often not what it seems: A Monticello-inspired folly can act as a focal point to a grassy path—and storage bin for a garden tools and supplies. Larger versions can serve as party spaces, the diminutive as hideaways for one or two. Others, outside the confines of the garden, are particularly special, like the redwood gazebo designed by William Turnbull Jr. and Mary Griffin. The structure sits high atop a hill, a secluded site for picnics.

Follies are not only the focus of the garden, but the focus of the gardener's imagination, site-poems that turn dross into dreams. Darina Allen, who heads the cooking school at Ireland's Ballymaloe House, discovered a use for the mountains of shells discarded by hardworking cooks and happy diners. Built among the inn's herb and vegetable gardens, a severe-looking folly opens to a reliquary of shells—an opalescent mosaic of mussels, scallops, clams and periwinkles.

objects

WILLIAM ROBINSON, THE LEGENDARY DEAN OF LATE-19TH-CENTURY ENGLISH garden writing, was at his most irascible when he considered his contemporaries' use of garden ornaments. "The dotting of statues," he complained, "is destructive of all repose." Considering the period's penchant for plopping neoclassical figures in most every nook and cranny of parks and estates—an unhappy affliction that can be seen even today in what one designer calls the "Big Houses"—one is tempted to agree.

Yet some of the most extraordinary gardens in the world are extraordinary precisely because of objects: Think of that most famous of all Japanese gardens, Ryoan-Ji, a masterpiece in Zen abstraction with only 15 stones in a courtyard of carefully raked gravel.

As Sir George Sitwell suggests, statues and other garden objects can

A question of scale: In a clearing in the woods on Cape Cod (opposite), bright, geometric sculptures by Allan Blank rise high above the informal garden planned by his wife, Chotsie, who chose hardy Shasta daisies and deep pink and red roses ('Showbiz', 'Betty Prior' and 'Bonica') for their strong color and low maintenance. Home-furnishings designer Bill Goldsmith did not let a 50-by-50-foot patio limit his plans (above). The Bay Area garden is a lesson in containment, almost entirely composed of pots filled with lobelia, iceplant, succulents, and a yew topiary, whose shape is echoed by a wooden finial.

"compel attention, stir imagination, strengthen memory, banish the consciousness of self and all trivial and obsessive thoughts." A tall order, but one which can be filled, as long as the object interacts with the overall design of the garden: Consider a bust made ethereal by the green light of a hornbeam tunnel, such as one at Netherland's Hetloo Palace. Or the optical high jinks of a water jar at the end of Jack Lenor Larsen's azalea walk, appearing—thanks to context—much larger than it actually is. The play of light, the manipulation of space, the precise placement of an object—all can contribute to the fictional wonder of the garden.

The types of objects one can use are as varied as gardens. Unfortunately, those offered in catalogues tend to be winged putti and copies of other scantily clad neoclassical figures, decorations now so hackneyed that their presence in a garden would most certainly fail to meet any of Sitwell's criteria. Bear in mind that the Persians, those most extraordinary early gardeners, never used graven images. Modern statues' abstract forms can act as a foil against nature's frills, and depending on the material used, even bring light into the garden. In smaller gardens, *objets trouvés*—the capital of a large column, a fragment of a windmill—engage the viewer's imagination, making proscribed boundaries disappear.

Statues can personify a garden. In Peggy McDonnell's fanciful New Jersey vegetable beds (opposite), an eight-foot-tall flowerpot scarecrow with petunia dreadlocks presides over the onion patch. Traditional statues that would be out of place in a rustic setting are at home in formal gardens at La Casella, the French Riviera home of Tom Parr and Claus Scheinert (above). The white limestone figure coaxes the visitor to look from one garden room into another.

How to choose? Usually it's best to select objects once the garden is established, taking cues from grounds and house: A small garden like the one designed by Bill Goldsmith would be overwhelmed by a large figurative statue. On the other hand, his minute globes and pyramids would be lost trinkets in a larger landscape.

Objects should contribute to the overall design of the garden. In some instances, they help create a sense of volume, as an antique lightning rod does, towering over the relatively flat vegetable garden of Bunny Williams. In others, they set a mood—serene, whimsical, intriguing, playful. For the amusement of dinner guests (and to the dismay of his more sedate neighbors), on the night of the party architect Richard Bergmann has been known to install a flock of pink plastic flamingoes leading from the street to his terrace garden. Whether modern or classical, flamboyant or sedate, permanent or transitory, the successful object should always achieve what Hugh Johnson describes as "the command to look."

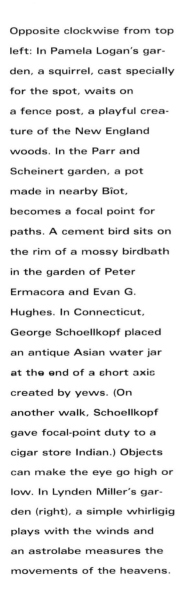

Opposite clockwise from top
left: In Pamela Logan's garden, a squirrel, cast specially
for the spot, waits on
a fence post, a playful creature of the New England
woods. In the Parr and
Scheinert garden, a pot
made in nearby Bîot,
becomes a focal point for
paths. A cement bird sits on
the rim of a mossy birdbath
in the garden of Peter
Ermacora and Evan G.
Hughes. In Connecticut,
George Schoellkopf placed
an antique Asian water jar
at the end of a short axis
created by yews. (On
another walk, Schoellkopf
gave focal-point duty to a
cigar store Indian.) Objects
can make the eye go high or
low. In Lynden Miller's garden (right), a simple whirligig
plays with the winds and
an astrolabe measures the
movements of the heavens.

seats

THE GARDEN SEAT HAS A TRIPARTATE ROLE: AS A PLACE TO SIT; AS SCULPTURE; and as a way of placing the viewer in a position to stop, look, listen, and smell.

The first and most obvious role is, in many instances, the most overlooked. Few benches—be they Italian neoclassical marble or modern wire—are comfortable enough to invite long periods of rest, unless softened with cushions. (Some, like the lacy cast-iron fripperies of the 1870s, will no doubt permanently cripple anyone foolish enough to tarry.) When choosing seating, consider the use: If it is to be poolside, on a sunny veranda, or overlooking some site set aside for picnickers, readers, and other outside bodies at rest, comfort should be a primary consideration.

In its second incarnation a seat should—like other garden sculpture—sit comfortably in its site. A rustic Adirondack chair will stand out as much in a formal garden as a backwoodsman would at a Park Avenue charity ball: Unless such a Hollywood effect is desired, the seating style should suit the garden style. At the same time, it should be as original as

possible. A seat carved out of a rocky promontory initiates the stroller into the essence of the site. An herbal bench with an earthen seat planted in thyme and head and armrests of chamomile, sweetly shaded with a canopy of climbing roses, is an attraction itself.

The third, and most important role, determines the seat's site. Focused on a grand vista, secluded in a private glade, or nestled under a fragrant lilac hedge, the seat's setting is so important that, in many instances, it should be included in garden plans.

More than just places to sit, benches help set the tone of a garden. Along a grassy hydrangea walk in Robert Meltzer's garden, under a wave of privet, a weathered bench is large enough for friends to sit comfortably (opposite). Even if strollers are too busy to stop, they can imagine the repose it promises. A wooden chaise, trim as a swimmer (right), nestles in a niche in a freestone wall, just a few feet from the pool at Charlotte Moss's eastern Long Island home, and a few inches away from urns filled with scented geraniums and petunias that encourage sweet repose. Plump white cushions can quickly be brought in when thunder warns of an approaching summer storm. The bench is light enough to be stored easily at summer's end.

Benches should be site specific. At Renny Reynolds' Pennsylvania farm, a bench of horizontal white metal bars encircles an an old tree (above). In the garden of Mark Hampton (left), the exaggerated back of a concave bench acts as a trellis. More sculpture than seating, a mossy English stone bench in Bunny Williams' garden (opposite) gives a sense of age and tranquility.

Seats can be visual cues to a garden's character, while offering olfactory temptations. Some suggest a sunny rusticity, like the faded painted bench in garden designer Judy Horton's herb garden (above left). Others encapsulate the sights and smells of Provence, as does a 19th-century cast-iron chair at the Saint-Remy farmhouse of Pierre Bergé (below left). Opposite, clockwise from top left: A rusted metal bench sets up a shadowy sense of intrigue and times gone by in Michael Trapp's terraced garden. A weathered teak bench spent many leisurely Nantucket summers in another garden before being sold at a tag sale and coming to rest at the end of one of the gravel paths in Rita and Samuel Robert's island garden. Daisies make a floral backdrop for a Victorian cast-iron bench, painted white in Chotsie Blank's Cape Cod garden. In San Miguel de Allende, the putti resting atop the stone bench, a copy of a Colonial period European bench, have a cheerful Hispaño accent.

garden + house

the site garden

AT FIRST GLIMPSE, THE SITE GARDEN DOES NOT APPEAR TO BE A GARDEN AT ALL. Lacking the elements we have come to expect—formal beds of flowers, clipped hedges, walls, linear walks—the site garden is often mistaken for a particularly exquisite example of the natural landscape, a bit of land blessed with beauty. In fact, the site garden is very much a garden designed to take full advantage of the natural assets of its location. Plans for such a garden are highly sensitive to the environment and make special use of native plant species and materials. Despite their untouched appearance, some of these landscapes are thoroughly man-made, their construction requiring quite as much hard work as more traditional gardens and considerably more finesse, since their success lies in hiding all evidence of human intervention. One of the last century's finest examples of such authorless design is Central Park, the green heart of Manhattan, 65 acres in which every tree, every meadow, every rock outcropping was planned by its justly famous designers, Frederick Law Olmsted and Calvert Vaux.

In the West, this style of gardening came to the fore in the early 18th century as the English Landscape School. Following Alexander Pope's dictum, "Consult the Genius of the Place in All," designers created ideal "naturalistic" landscapes—either pastoral (gentle meadows, grazing cows or sheep, placid ponds) or picturesque (intentionally wild vistas). One of the period's most esteemed practitioners, Capability Brown (who got his name from seeing the "capabilities" of the landscape), believed that nature tended toward the ideal, but sometimes failed to reach that ideal because of accidents. It was his job to correct "Nature's mistakes," turning a bog

A crystalline box, Philip
Johnson's Glass House
seems to encase the
Connecticut landscape.
A carpet of grass, bound
by a low ribbon of stone,
extends from the house to
a precipice overlooking the
Rippowam Valley. In fact,
the pastoral setting was
a tangle of dense growth
when Johnson bought the
land in 1946, so dense the
architect began "organizing
the woods."

into a pastoral setting with a pond and new winding river, thinning a dense woodland to reveal a view of a manor house. So famous was Capability that his work was mentioned in a play: "Aye, Styx," one character proclaimed. "Why 'tis as straight as Fleet Ditch. You should have given it a serpentine sweep, and sloped the banks of it. The place indeed has fine *capabilities*; but you should clear the wood to the left and clump the trees on the right."

Although such work sounds extravagant, landscape architects today are doing many of the same things, albeit on a slightly less grand scale. As A.E. Bye—one of the nation's leading exponents of this subtle art—more humbly puts it, he takes "inspiration directly from existing conditions."

Bye, and other landscape architects like him, work to find the spirit of the place, and to intensify or highlight some aspect of nature through the use of native plants, materials, and organic design. When skillfully crafted, such a landscape often leads the casual viewer to think the owner very lucky to have happened on such a remarkable site. "It has often been the story of my work that one never knows I've done anything," Bye has said.

Shaping such an understated landscape requires an intimate knowledge of the site and its ecosystem. It also demands a poetic imagination to recognize the full potential of the site: A decision not to put a house on the top of a hill, but on a lower butte, or to realize a depression could make a fine pond. The house is often an integral part of the site garden, seeming to spring organically from the land. Once the house is built, herculean efforts are frequently required to make the structure look as if it had always been there—carpets of native mosses are rolled out to cover the disturbed ground, and trees are planted to replace those that had been cut down.

And although some practitioners like James Cutler go to great lengths not to cut trees, others who are Capability Brown's heirs will chop away to reveal the essence of the landscape. To make a pastoral setting for his own home, Philip Johnson engaged in a process he called "negative landscaping"—a relentless removal of trees that provoked neighbors' polite protest. Once all this unseen work is finished, the site garden becomes part of the natural landscape, a self-sustaining work of art.

On the gently rolling, rich farmland of Wisconsin, a whimsical
architectural creature crouches
beside a stand of hardwood
trees. In his design, Turner
Brooks, a Connecticut-based
architect, borrowed the Crayola
colors—candy-cane striped
board-and-batten and creamy
yellow clapboard—from neighboring Norwegian-style barns.
Amos Miller, a sculptor and
artist, and Sharon Lombard, a
designer and performance
artist, decided their land should
blend in with the agrarian
scenery. Miller plowed and lev-
eled the land around their house
and planted it with a basic crop
of grass and alfalfa. The only
"gardening" he does comes
when he mows a semi-circle of
pasture after the wild daisies
and Queen Anne's lace have
flowered and gone to seed. In
the spring, plum and apple trees
(some original to the 160-acre
farm, some saplings) bloom into
sweet-smelling clouds.

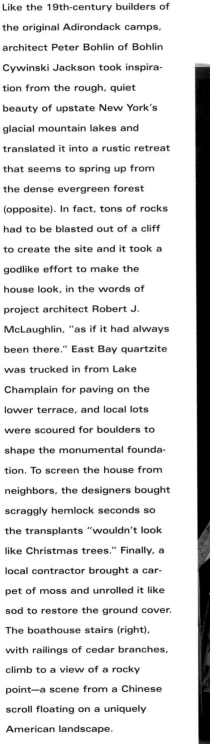

Like the 19th-century builders of the original Adirondack camps, architect Peter Bohlin of Bohlin Cywinski Jackson took inspiration from the rough, quiet beauty of upstate New York's glacial mountain lakes and translated it into a rustic retreat that seems to spring up from the dense evergreen forest (opposite). In fact, tons of rocks had to be blasted out of a cliff to create the site and it took a godlike effort to make the house look, in the words of project architect Robert J. McLaughlin, "as if it had always been there." East Bay quartzite was trucked in from Lake Champlain for paving on the lower terrace, and local lots were scoured for boulders to shape the monumental foundation. To screen the house from neighbors, the designers bought scraggly hemlock seconds so the transplants "wouldn't look like Christmas trees." Finally, a local contractor brought a carpet of moss and unrolled it like sod to restore the ground cover. The boathouse stairs (right), with railings of cedar branches, climb to a view of a rocky point—a scene from a Chinese scroll floating on a uniquely American landscape.

Noriko and Richard Moore—
she a weaver, he a graphic
designer—camped on their
property in rural Connecticut
most weekends for eight years
before they finally decided on
the site and type of house they
wanted. With the aid of Alfredo
De Vido, a New York City architect, and New York landscape
architect Edmund D. Hollander,
they fashioned a house that
virtually disappears into the hillside. Posts and beams were
milled from red oaks cut to clear
the site, and walls were laid
with fieldstones, about half of
which came from the site. In a
reverent bow to Yankee stone
fences, no mortar was used;
Christmas ferns and climbing
hydrangeas cling to the crev-
asses. De Vido designed a flat
earth-covered roof and planted
it with a slow-growing native
sedge commonly found along
New England roadsides. The
earth's mass helps maintain a
comfortable temperature inside
the house, while transforming
the roof into a succession of
grassy terraces. Underneath,
windows gaze south down a
wooded slope of pachysandra
(despised by deer) to a man-
made pond.

Following Frank Lloyd Wright's principle that a house should be of a hill, not on it, San Antonio architects Lake/Flato rejected a high promontory and selected instead a knoll above the Llano River as the site of Mark Chandler's ranch house (opposite). Limestone pillars—built of stone found on the land—jut up like natural outcroppings, supporting a galvanized metal roof that reflects the big Central Texas sky. Bearing in mind that this is a weekend retreat, landscape architect Jim Keeter selected flora that could survive with scant attention. In his indigenous plant palette Keeter included twisted leaf yucca and Texas sotol (right), whose tall spiky leaves lacerate the landscape. He countered their harsh geometries with furry-leafed lamb's ear and enlivened the hardscrabble landscape with bright pink skullcap, purple coneflowers, brazen blackfoot daisies, and ox-eye daisies. A decomposed granite drive curves through native buffalo grass, which Keeter also planted on a level stretch of land close by the river, along with river fern and fox-red curly sedum.

Before James Cutler sits down
to his drafting table to design,
the Winslow, Washington, architect walks a site for at least 10
hours: "I want to discover the
best qualities of the land, and
then organize the architecture
to reveal those qualitites." This
is exactly what he did when
John and Elinor Paulk asked him
to design a home for them on a
wooded site on the Olympic
Peninsula (opposite). His
response was a glorious tree
house on stilts (to give the first
floor a view of the Hood Canal).
A 127-foot-long ramp 15 feet off
the ground shoots from the
parking area in front of the
house (above right) through to
the back, where it ends with a
bird's-eye view of the water and
the third-growth forest with its
20-foot rhododendron and large
huckleberries (below right). "He
wanted our house to look as if
it had dropped there out of
heaven," said John Paulk. To
help heaven, a red alder thicket
was planted, a colonizing tree
that also makes the earth more
fertile. Cutler tries to avoid
destroying trees and plants. "I
am sick of killing things," Cutler
says emphatically. When possible, original firs and alders were
replanted; a hand axe was used
on the few trees that weren't.

perfect union

IN THE FEBRUARY 1902 ISSUE OF HOUSE BEAUTIFUL, READERS WERE TREATED
to this description of "A Successful House in England": "From every point
on the land from which it can be seen, the house seems to grow out of the
ground." The story goes on to comment on the south terrace, where a
"double flight of wide easy steps" leads to the garden, the scheme of
which "has been kept very simple. It was evident that the beautiful stretch
of forest ground deserved to have its own sentiment preserved as much as
possible."

The writer was the famed English gardener Gertrude Jekyll; the
architect, her esteemed collaborator Edwin Lutyens. The partnership was
such a felicitous one, the skill of each enhancing the work of the other, that
to this day their combined efforts set a standard for the union between
house and garden.

"It is upon the right relation of the garden to the house that its value
and the enjoyment that is to be derived from it will largely depend," Jekyll
wrote elsewhere. "The connection must be intimate, and the access not
only convenient but inviting." Although the reigning styles of architecture
and gardens have changed many times since, the principles remain.

In this section, we consider five houses and gardens, each of which
attempts that intimate connection. In some instances, the gardens have
been grafted onto an existing house, happy late marriages. In others, as in

the instance of the home of Buzz Yudell and Tina Beebe, the influence of the Lutyens/Jekyll architect/garden-designer team is clearly present. Although the southern California "moonscape" Yudell and Beebe transformed differs vastly from the English countryside, their attention to geography and site and their use of intermediary spaces are exactly the tools employed by the Adam and Eve of modern Western gardening.

Relating the design of the garden to the house does not necessarily mean something as obvious as matching English cottage gardens with English cottages. Indeed, the type of garden appropriate to a specific house has as much to do with the personality of the gardener, the climate, and the culture of the times as with any particular architectural style: Consider the Cubist garden designed by Gabriel Guévrékian in the 1920s for Robert Mallet-Stevens' avant-garde Villa Noailles in Hyères, or the brilliant bougainvillea-clad terraces that Richard Neutra pencilled in on plans for his International Style houses of the 1930s and 1940s. Perfect unions are not prosaic.

William Robinson wrote: "The union between the house beautiful and the ground near it . . . should interest men more and more as our cities grow larger and our lovely English landscape shrinks back from them." His sentiments—robustly argued over a century ago—are as true for our times and our land as they were for his.

For generations the intimate connection between garden and house has been the aim of great gardeners and architects, as evidenced in a manor house designed by Edwin Lutyens and gardens by Gertrude Jekyll, (opposite), and in Robert Mallet-Stevens' Villa Noailles (above).

One of the first parts of the Connecticut garden Bunny Williams reworked was the entry, replacing a path of "ugly blue stones" with antique bricks, more in keeping with what the designer calls the "chaste New England front." Alternating round clipped boxwoods and Italian terra-cotta pots, brimming with a different annual every year, set up a subtle rhythm along the straight walk (opposite). Williams serves breakfast and lunch on the loggia off the kitchen (above). For the broad floor, she specified antique brick worked in a basket-weave pattern. Just outside, the bold, vertical shapes of three clipped yews break the long horizontal mass of the wing.

splendored rooms

WHEN INTERIOR DESIGNER BUNNY WILLIAMS BOUGHT HER house in northwest Connecticut in 1978, it was a neglected boarding house. The interior designer was not fazed: "I loved the idea of rescuing it."

It had good—if historically rather mixed—bones. The original farmhouse, now the dining room, dates from 1780. An addition in grander Federal style reconfigured the house in 1840. In the 1930s, a second story materialized above the carriage house (now, among other things, the kitchen, mud room, and loggia). "This house had a split personality," she noted. "A chaste New England front, and then this totally abandoned back."

Given Williams' proclivities, it comes as little surprise that the back is no longer totally abandoned, but an elegant, formally organized garden which, like her home, has evolved in stages.

Tackling the garden the way she does interiors, Williams created rooms defined by "walls"—at the back, a six-foot-tall hemlock hedge; on the sides,

A fieldstone wall transformed the sloping back lawn into a terrace and sunken garden (opposite above). Williams framed the reflecting pool with granite, which she also used as steps and tops of walls. To create a space within a space, she later added four columns, painted gray like the lattice that defines the side borders. Past the pool, an arbor flanked by two old crabapple trees leads to a meadow; a Tuscan oil jar acts as a focal point (opposite below and above left). Small details count: Williams had a woodworker copy a Federal finial to ornament the lattice fences (above right).

lattice fences with broad borders of annuals and perennials. (The use of lattice, which Williams also incorporated in the arbor "door" of the hedge and lattice columns around the pool, is an example of how she integrated house and garden.) She reworked the garden's "ceiling," trimming away branches of a 250-year-old maple so that more sunlight would filter onto the lawn.

Taking her cue from the gently sloping land behind her house, Williams divided the space into two levels with a retaining wall built of fieldstone purchased from a nearby farm. She topped the wall with specially cut granite slabs, fine surfaces for her legions of potted plants, and used the same granite as risers for broad steps leading from the grass terrace to the sunken garden and as a frame for the reflecting pool, which she sited in the sunniest part of the garden.

Other "rooms" followed: a multi-hued cutting garden/vegetable patch that, in addition to providing bounteous fare for the table, acts as a bright counterpoint to the restrained soft colors of the rest of the garden; a loggia for meals; a formal potager near the barn; and, most recently, a woodland garden. "It's just like working on the house," Williams reflected. "You get one part under control, and then you go on to the next, always tying it back to the original house, to make it look as if it always belonged."

sag harbor spirit

N Sag Harbor, New York, on a quiet street between the wharf where whaling ships once anchored and the old cemetery where markers commemorate captains and mates lost at sea, stands the weekend home of interior designer Robert K. Lewis and his family. The 1868 structure is just one of many 18th- and 19th-century houses in the National Historic District that encompasses the heart of the village.

Over the past two decades, the town has become a favored summering spot of Manhattanites. The newcomers hurried to give face-lifts to these handsome houses and their grounds, and Lewis was no exception, tackling the house and garden with an inexorable enthusiasm. To keep in the spirit of the bayside village, Lewis had the shingled house painted putty with white trim. He then dug up a side yard (really an extra lot, 50 by 150 feet—a great luxury in the village) and laid it out, from front to back, along a long walkway of brick, a descendant of the old brick walk that skips and bumps its way past the Old Whaler's Church down the street. For a short time, Lewis followed village tradition, ordering boxwood hedges from a local nursery and fencing the front with picket and privet, and then

In an old whaling village on Long Island, designer Robert K. Lewis has taken a side lawn and made it into three formal garden rooms along a brick walk. The open side porch (opposite) is a fine place for people-watching and smelling the scent of roses, including Lewis's favorite, 'Abraham Darby'. The "room" closest to the street is the rose garden (above), where pea-gravel paths lined with brick intersect at an iron urn filled with pansies and balanced on a brick pedestal.

The brick path runs along the house, ending in a patio surrounded by clipped boxwoods in large terra-cotta pots (opposite). Here, the Lewis family enjoys casual meals. Immediately to the rear is a Gothic folly, where vines will eventually provide shade from the hot summer sun. Farthest from the street is the kitchen garden (above), a checkerboard of herbs and salad greens, ending in a postage stamp of grass. The tepees are supports for snow peas or tomatoes, depending on the season.

he broke it, dividing the open yard into three very formal spaces which act as outdoor extensions of the house.

Closest to the street is the rose "room," filled with David Austin roses underplanted with pinks and lavender. A lead Victorian urn on a brick pedestal dominates the nexus of the gravel paths.

In the central section, running alongside the porch, are diamond-shaped beds, slightly raised and rimmed with brick, overflowing with Victorian favorites—summersweet, franklinia, morning glories, plume poppy, and blue-flowering chaste tree—mixed with gray-foliage foreground plants, such as white *Nicotiana sylvestris*.

Farthest from the street is the kitchen garden, 16 raised wood beds of various herbs, salad greens, and scented plants—an ever-changing still-life for the outdoor dining table on the nearby brick terrace. Behind this, close to an old apple tree (about all that is left of the old garden), is a Gothic gazebo, more a tribute to Lewis's imagination than to village history. It stands on the only patch of lawn left—a lawn that may not last long: "I hardly have any space left to plant," sighed the eager gardener, "so I'll have to jump to the next square."

bucks county hybrid

Flagstones unearthed outside Renny Reynolds' 18th-century Pennsylvania stone house were reconfigured into a path along the front, lined with moss and lightened with impatiens (opposite). Nearby, a Cinderella-esque transformation changed a milk shed into a peacock house. On the south side (above) an American tradition is preserved: A porch is a screened haven in summer and a windowed sunroom that brightens inclement months.

ALMOST TWO DECADES AFTER RENNY REYNOLDS and Jack Staub bought Boxwood—their 72-acre estate in Bucks County—the farmhouse is just what one imagines a Pennsylvania fieldstone Colonial should be: a genteel assembly of three 18th-century structures encompassing gracious rooms restored with care and finesse (Reynolds scraped the pine panelling in the dining room down to what is known locally as "original blue," a stain made of blueberry juice) and furnished with Delaware Valley antiques. Across the back of the main house a screened porch stretches, long as a summer's day, overlooking grass that flows to a stream and gemlike pond. In the front, Reynolds (who is a member of the local Heritage Conservancy) continued his quest for regional authenticity, clipping back tangles of boxwoods into a string of spheres and filling the gaps with feathery ostrich ferns. With the

enthusiasm of an amateur archeologist, he unearthed cut flagstones outside the original 1723 Quaker house and reworked his find into a terrace and a walk that leads to the main entrance in the 1793 section.

Shedding his plain Quaker coat, Reynolds embraced the rest of the 17 acres with the flamboyantly romantic imagination that has made him one of New York's most celebrated floral and party designers. Some of his party props wind up as centerpieces in his landscape tableaux. A 500-foot perennial border runs between two barns and down to a circular pool.

The garden is a daybook of his European travels: A stay with Christopher Lloyd at Great Dixter resulted in the purchase of a cache of bellflowers; a recent foray to Paris' *Marché aux Puces* yielded a treasure trove of garden furniture. "I am a collector—I get inspiration for my work and for my garden wherever I go," Reynolds explained.

To link the back lawn to the lily and fern gardens, Reynolds built an arching cement bridge (left) faced with stones from the creek and "paved" with sod. A similar car bridge with traditional paving crosses upstream, close to the pond that the ever-enterprising designer created by digging to bedrock and letting the stream fill the depression. Reynolds—pictured taking a brief rest with his dogs on the folly in the pond (opposite)—says that he had originally intended to cover the peaked roof with cedar shake, but realized that the open framework created a delightful tracery for sunlight and welcome summer breezes. Beyond the edge of the pond, fringed with a mixture of wild daylilies and cultivars, a dirt path weaves through the forest. Once rampant with poison ivy and wild grapevines, the woodland garden is now an Eden of hostas and other shade-loving plants where strollers are tempted with rustic seats and benches.

inside/out

WHEN LOS ANGELES INTERIOR DECORATOR SUSAN STRING-
fellow asked architects Susan Lanier and Paul Lubowicki
to draw up plans to expand her Spanish Colonial Revival
house, she knew that she did not want an addition that
mimicked John Byers' 1920s design, but rather a crisp,
modern space that would preserve the integrity and feeling of the original. "We wanted a dialogue between old and new, not a debate," said
Lubowicki.

A similar dialogue was engaged in the garden designed by Nancy
Goslee Power. Stringfellow, according to Power, "had always thought of the
house and garden as a single, harmonious composition, with little distinc-
tion between inside and outside." In the addition, clerestories, glass doors,
and windows extending to the floor opened the house to the garden.

In the master bedroom (left)
the swath of lavender
makes green and purple
bands that are only briefly
interrupted by a supporting
wall and the fireplace.
Looking at the house from
the field of lavender (opposite), only the new addition
is visible (from the front,
only the old house can be
seen). A path of decom-
posed granite trickles back
to a circle an old pomegranate tree before it meets a
stone terrace separated
from the dining room only by
glass doors. The architects
used a variety of fenestra-
tion to open the indoor
space to the outdoors: A tri-
angular window that follows
the roofline gives a view of
the tall eucalyptus.

A pomegranate tree
marks the line between
the terrace full of lavender
that stretches to the
Mediterranean border
garden beyond (opposite).
The back terrace, with its
patterned concrete wall,
functions as an outdoor
room (above left), while the
formal front courtyard
retains much of its original
character (right), with wand-
like buttonhole orchids
(*Epidendrum ibaguense*)
echoing the orange tiles in
a wall mosaic.

Outside, the linkage was continued by extending the dining room past the glass doors to a stone terrace which dissolved into a stepping-stone path encircling a gnarled pomegranate tree. Power positioned a water-lily pool, slightly off the central axis of the house so "the reflection can be seen from almost every room."

As in the addition, the materials used in the garden are limited in number, but elegant. Paths of decomposed granite (light in color, echoing the plaster walls of both old and new sections of the house) run diagonally into a sea of lavender (*Lavandula multifida*) that reaches what Power calls a "sunny, Mediterranean border": purple flowering Pride of Madeira, cranesbill, *aster Frikartii*, Jerusalem sage (*Phlomis fruticosa*), white Matilija poppies (*Romneya coulteri*), and chartreuse *Euphorbia characias* 'wulfenii'.

In the front garden, close attention was paid to retaining the original lines and plantings. Using old bricks, Power linked the rear garden to the entry courtyard by extending an old narrow driveway. More buttonhole orchids and green saucer plants were added to existing communities, and a new wall became home to two espaliered Australian tea trees.

mediterranean muse

THE 100-BY-600-FOOT RECTANGULAR PLOT IN THE FOOTHILLS OF THE Santa Monica Mountains had been the perfect shape for the land's first incarnation as a tomato farm (all the easier to plough). But as a home and garden site, the possibilities were pinched. Tina Beebe and Robert (Buzz) Yudell—entranced by the panoramic views of the Pacific and the fine, alluvial dirt—decided to accent the negative, and slithered a California version of a Tuscan farmhouse onto the narrow site.

Using strong, geometric shapes, Yudell, partner in the architectural firm Moore Ruble Yudell, designed a home that followed the gentle slope of the land. Living spaces open onto a long gallery; French doors swing out onto a wide cascade of stairs that culminates in a pool. Taking advantage of the Southern California climate, the couple designed a series of "streets" across the stairs from these doors, terraces with gardens and outdoor rooms framed with airy pergolas.

As if to remind visitors of the land's agrarian heritage, wild strawberries (*Fragaria vesca*) break through Vicenza limestone at the front entry (above). From there, stairs cascade down the 7-percent grade and spill into a pool at the south end of the property (opposite). Here the air is sweet with the scents of yellow angel's-trumpet and geraniums.

French doors open off the gallery running the length of the house to a series of terraced streets with open-air rooms formed by pergolas (opposite). Holes in limestone pavers set in cement provide perfect growing conditions for poppies—oriental, Iceland, and corn—which break up what would otherwise be a relentless expanse of hardscape. Grapevines and climbing roses, including pink 'Shot Silk' and pale yellow 'Gloire de Dijon', decorate the walls and ceilings of outdoor rooms to the left of the stairs. These rooms and the pool's open cabana (above) offer fine spots for enjoying the breathtaking view of the Pacific.

Tina, an architectural colorist and (now) garden designer, was at first intimidated by the task: "It was like a moonscape," she said. Soon, she realized the site's possibilities, and with an Easterner's heady joy at the prospect of subtropical growing conditions, she anchored the property at its entrance to the south with an olive grove, and to the north with fig, pomegranate, quince, and peach trees.

Now the pergolas are twined with grapevines and roses underplanted with iris and heucheras. (Nearly three dozen English roses thrive here, fanned by the sea breezes.) Wild strawberries and salvias poke up through the Vicenza limestone walk, infusing the space with color and perfume. Originally Beebe and Yudell planned to use the costly Italian stone only around the pool, but when the merchant offered a low price on a palette of broken stones, they seized the opportunity and—once again—made art out of adversity.

Bowing to the region's low rainfall, Beebe planted a Mediterranean border in the lowest terrace, just above the pool, and turned the central outdoor sitting room into an open-air aviary with flowers beloved of humming birds—euphorbias, salvias, and penstemons. Meandering paths trickle to an end at the arroyo, atumble with chaparral plants such as ceanothus and California oak—natives that were here long before the farm.

riviera reverie

L A CASELLA—THE FRENCH RIVIERA HOME OF TOM PARR AND CLAUS Scheinert—is a magnificent example of how house and garden can be sublimely linked. It was to be expected that Parr, the former chairman of Colefax & Fowler, would turn the down-at-the-heels copy of Madame de Pompadour's pavilion at Fontainebleau into a place of assured grace and charm. It reflects, as he explained, "the essence of what I really love, without any compromises." The fact that Claus Scheinert, a retired businessman, created, in his first horticultural venture, one of the Riviera's finest new gardens is somewhat more surprising. Yet, like the interior of the house, the landscape reveals a love of pattern and design on a grand scale, combined with a fine eye for texture and detail.

Scheinert was inspired to resurrect the garden—with its overgrown hedges and weed-choked terraces—after visits to Villa Noailles and the Chèvre d'Or in Biôt. Without hesitation, he mixed English floral display with Italian perspectives formed by clipped cypress and cherry laurel hedges—some original, some newly planted. "I like the grandeur of a formal

When Tom Parr and Claus Scheinert bought La Casella in 1984, they worked in concert to connect the house to the garden, visually as well as thematically. A window in the salon (above left) looks west to a magnificent vista past the blue-and-white garden (above right) and cherry laurel columns down to the myrtle walk beyond. Parr and Scheinert removed ivy covering the exterior of the house (opposite) and did away with a swimming pool crowding the entry. On a lower level, Scheinert—who became resident gardener— replaced the pool with a koi pond set in a gravel terrace.

Throughout the garden, clipped evergreens establish a formal, symmetrical framework. A cypress hedge defines the entry terrace's eastern edge, while three towering cypress spires mirror a similar planting to the west (opposite). The flowing shape of a 400-year-old olive tree softens the strict geometry. Also to the west, small jets of water (above) create concentric ripples on a small canal—one of eight ponds. Espaliered lemon trees and balls of bougainvillea rise out of tufts of fragrant creeping rosemary.

garden, but that alone would be boring," he mused. "A garden of simply flowers and uncut trees and bushes would be too romantic, too untidy. And so I decided to do both." Only later did he realize that this very idea was at the heart of the work of British landscape architect Arabella Lennox-Boyd, whom he subsequently met and admires.

While Parr took down interior walls, opening the house to terraces he designed, Scheinert worked on the plantings. The first site to be reworked was just off the main terrace and to the west of the house. The blue-and-white garden—a dreamlike mixture of white-flowered hebes, nicotianas, geraniums, convolvulus, and blue-blossomed plumbagos, ceanothus, and agapanthus—established the garden's prevailing color palette. Only the cutting garden—near the vegetable plot, fruit orchard, and guest cottage at the entrance of the estate—varies, providing bright country bouquets.

Scheinert is quick to state that he never had a grand plan. Instead, over five years, he and Parr created a series of terraced gardens—10 in all. Elegantly hewn hedges and finely wrought walls divide and connect

With a steadfast enthusiasm and able gardeners, Scheinert cut old hedges and planted new to fashion rooms, corridors, and allées. To open the view on the west side of the house, Scheinert broke a solid hedge of cherry laurel into two columns that mark the entrance to the myrtle walk (left). An 18th-century statue of a lady stands patiently at the far end of a cypress allée. South of the main house, just past the entrance of the property, a guest cottage (opposite) is wreathed in white jasmine and wisteria. Off its small terrace, gardeners clipped a cypress house with a window at the peak, creating a vernal room enlivened with lavender and yellow *Fremontodendron californicum.*

the procession of elegant spaces, including the exquisite myrtle walk, a pink-and-white rose garden, and the fruit terrace with its cornucopia of apricot, plum, cherry, and greengage trees. No detail is overlooked: Beyond the koi pond a pair of statues—Autumn and Winter—engage in distant conversation, two of a host of 18th-century statuary found, quite by accident, at a château in Aix.

And so the garden has grown, terrace by terrace—here a lavender-lined grass walk leads to a weather-worn bench, a quiet spot for contemplation; there a pergola wreathed in white wisteria shades a stone dining table, a set for polite conversation. A work of modern-day alchemy, the romantic combinations of flowers and complex spatial relationships meld into a terrain that at once astounds and delights.

designer directory

BYRON BELL
BELL LARSON ARCHITECTS & PLANNERS
123 W. 3rd St.
New York, NY 10012
(212)995-5292

RICHARD BERGMANN ARCHITECTS
63 Park St.
New Canaan, CT 06840
(203)966-9505

BARRY A. BERKUS
B3 ARCHITECTS/BERKUS DESIGN STUDIO
2020 Alameda Padre Serra
Santa Barbara, CA 93103
(805)966-1547

PETER BOHLIN
BOHLIN CYWINSKI JACKSON
182 N. Franklin St.
Wilkes-Barre, PA 18701
(717)825-8756

DALE BOOHER AND LISA STAMM
THE HOMESTEAD GARDEN AND DESIGN
COLLABORATIVE
P.O. Box 90
Shelter Island, NY 11965
(516)749-2189

TURNER BROOKS
235 Lawrence St.
New Haven, CT 06511
(203)787-2234

A.E. BYE
158 Danbury Rd.
Ridgefield, CT 06877
(203)431-4646

JON CARLOFTIS AND WILLIS WATTS
DESIGN 6 LANDSCAPE
P.O. Box 57
Erwinna, PA 18920
(610)294-8057

JAMES CUTLER ARCHITECTS
135 Parfitt Way SW
Bainbridge, WA 98110
(206)842-4710

JAMES DEGREY DAVID AND GARY PEESE
GARDENS
1818 W. 35th St.
Austin, Texas 78703
(512)451-5490

ALFREDO DE VIDO ARCHITECTS
1044 Madison Ave.
New York, NY 10024
(212)517-6100

ANTHONY ELLIOTT
Snug Harbor Farm
87 Western Ave.
Kennebunk, ME 04043
(207)967-2414

RYAN GAINEY & CO.
2973 Hardman Court
Atlanta, GA 30305
(404)233-2050

TURNBULL GRIFFIN HAESLOOP ARCHITECTS
Pier 1 1/2
The Embarcadero
San Francisco, CA 94111
(415)986-3642

GARDEN OF DAVID HICKS
The Grove
Brightwell Baldwin
Oxfordshire OX95PF
England
011-44-14-91-824-555

JUDY M. HORTON AND CHERYL K. LERNER
JUDY M. HORTON GARDEN DESIGN
256 S. Van Ness
Los Angeles, CA 90004
(323)933-0501

THE JOHN P. HUMES JAPANESE STROLL GARDEN
P.O.Box 671
Locust Valley, NY 11560
(516)676-4486

RAYMOND JUNGLES INC.
517 Duval St., #206
Key West, FL 33040
(305)294-6700

JIM KEETER
J.E.K., INC.
P.O. Box 691090
San Antonio, TX 78269
(210)698-0083

JACK LENOR LARSEN
LongHouse Reserve
133 Hands Creek Rd.
East Hampton, NY 11937
(516)329-3568

SUSAN LANIER AND PAUL LUBOWICKI
LUBOWICKI/LANIER ARCHITECTS
337 Kansas St., Unit A
El Segundo, CA 90245
(310)322-0211

Ron Lutsko Jr.
Lutsko Associates
Pier 1/2
The Embarcadero
San Francisco, CA 94111
(415)391-0777

Hitch Lyman
P.O. Box 591
Trumansburg, NY 14886
(607)272-8165

Nancy McCabe
163 Dublin Rd.
Falls Village, CT 06031
(203)824-0354

Lynden B. Miller Public Garden Design
New York, NY

Charlotte Moss & Co.
16 E. 65th St.
New York, NY 10021
(212)734-7250

Oehme, van Sweden & Associates
800 G St., SE
Washington D.C. 20003
(202)546-7575

Ben Page & Associates LLC
1206 17th Ave., South
Nashville, TN 37212
(615)327-0220

Nancy Goslee Power & Associates
1660 Stanford St.
Santa Monica, CA 90404
(310)264-0266

Renny Reynolds and Jack Staub
505 Park Ave.
New York, NY 10022
(212)288-7000

Mark Rudkin
BP29 Le Mesnil
St. Denis, France
011-33-34619909

Erica Shank Photography
P.O. Box 993
Amagansett, NY 11930

Jim and Beverley Thompson
45330 Duxbury Rd.
Manchester, CA 95459
(707)882-2345

Michael Trapp
7 River Road, Box 67
West Cornwall, CT 06796
(800)672-6098

Edwina vonGal
442-24 9th St.
Long Island City, NY 11101
(718)706-6007

Bunny Williams
Treillage
418 E. 75th St.
New York, NY 10021
(212)535-2288

Jacques Wirtz
Wirtz International
Botermelkdijk 464, B-2900
Schoten, Belgium
011-323-680-1322

Marcy Li Wong Architects
2251 5th St.
Berkeley, CA 94710
(510)843-0916

Donn Logan
ELS/Elbasani & Logan Architects
2040 Addison St.
Berkeley, CA 94704
(510)549-2929

Buzz Yudell and Tina Beebe
Moore Ruble Yudell
933 Pico Blvd.
Santa Monica, CA 90405
(310)450-1400

Zion & Breen Associates
The Mill
33 Imlaystown Rd.,
P.O. Box 34
Imlaystown, NJ 08526
(609)259-9555

To obtain information about visiting
gardens nationwide, contact:
THE GARDEN CONSERVANCY
P.O. Box 219
Cold Spring, NY 10516
(914)265-2029

photography credits

1   JOHN HALL (BEN PAGE DESIGN)

2   JOHN HALL (ROBERT MELTZER GARDEN)

3   JOHN HALL (ROBERT MELTZER GARDEN)

8   JULIE MARIS/SEMEL (ELIOT CLARKE GARDEN)

11   RICHARD FELBER (LYNDEN MILLER GARDEN)

14   JOSHUA GREEN (JIM & BEVERLY THOMPSON GARDEN)

16   JOHN HALL

17   JOHN HALL

18   JOHN HALL

19   JOHN HALL

20-21   JOHN HALL

22   RICHARD FELBER

23   RICHARD FELBER

24   RICHARD FELBER

25   RICHARD FELBER

26   RICHARD FELBER

27   RICHARD FELBER

28   RICHARD FELBER

29   RICHARD FELBER

30   RICHARD FELBER

31   RICHARD FELBER

32-33   RICHARD FELBER

34   L.Q. YOUNKERS

35   L.Q. YOUNKERS

36   L.Q. YOUNKERS

37   L.Q. YOUNKERS

38   L.Q. YOUNKERS

40   JOSHUA GREEN

41   JOSHUA GREEN

42-43   JOSHUA GREEN

44   JOSHUA GREEN

45   JOSHUA GREEN

47   JOSHUA GREEN

48   KEN DRUSE

49   KEN DRUSE

50   KEN DRUSE

51   KEN DRUSE

52   KEN DRUSE

53   KEN DRUSE

54   RICHARD FELBER

56   RICHARD FELBER

57   RICHARD FELBER

58   RICHARD FELBER

59   RICHARD FELBER

60   KEN DRUSE

61   KEN DRUSE

62   KEN DRUSE

63   KEN DRUSE

65   KEN DRUSE

66   KAREN BUSSOLINI

67   KAREN BUSSOLINI

68   KAREN BUSSOLINI

69   KAREN BUSSOLINI

70   KAREN BUSSOLINI

72   JOHN HALL

73   JOHN HALL

75   JOHN HALL

76   JOHN HALL

77   JOHN HALL

78   JOHN HALL

80   KEN DRUSE

81   KEN DRUSE

82   KEN DRUSE

83   KEN DRUSE

84-85   KEN DRUSE

86   KEN DRUSE

87   KEN DRUSE

88   KEN DRUSE

89   KEN DRUSE

90   KEN DRUSE (SHANK GARDEN)

92-93   LIZZIE HIMMEL

94   ROB GRAY (TOP LEFT)

94   THIBAULT JEANSON (TOP RIGHT)

94   KATHLENE PERSOFF (BOTTOM LEFT)

94   DOMINIQUE VORILLON (BOTTOM RIGHT)

96   DOMINIQUE VORILLON

97   TIM STREET-PORTER

98   SCOTT FRANCES

99   MICHAEL MUNDY

100   JOHN VAUGHAN

101   RICHARD FELBER

102   DOMINIQUE VORILLON (TOP)

102   THIBAULT JEANSON (BOTTOM)

103   TIM STREET-PORTER (TOP)

103   MICHAEL DUNNE (BOTTOM)

104   ©MARK DARLEY/ESTO

105   RICHARD FELBER

106-107   TIM STREET-PORTER

108   ERICA LENNARD

109   RICHARD FELBER

110   JOHN HALL

111   CURTICE TAYLOR

112   CLAIRE DE VIRIEU

113   CURTICE TAYLOR (TOP LEFT, BOTTOM RIGHT & LEFT)

113   DANA HYDE (TOP RIGHT)

114   FAITH ECHTEMEYER

116   BRIAN VANDEN BRINK

117   JEFF MCNAMARA

118   JOHN HALL (TOP)

118   PETER MARGONELLI (BOTTOM)

119   ROBERT STARKOFF

120   DANA HYDE (TOP)

120   JOHN HALL (BOTTOM)

121   MICK HALES

123   KEN DRUSE (TOP LEFT, BOTTOM RIGHT)

123   WILLIAM WALDRON (TOP RIGHT)

123   CUTICE TAYLOR (BOTTOM LEFT)

124   THIBAULT JEANSON (TOP)

124   KEN DRUSE (BOTTOM)

125   JOHN HALL (TOP)

125   KEN DRUSE (BOTTOM)

126   JOHN HALL

129   RICHARD MARTIN (TOP)

129   LANGDON CLAY (BOTTOM)

131   CURTICE TAYLOR

132   PETER MARGONELLI

133   KEN DRUSE

134   KATHLENE PERSOFF

135   JESSE GERNSTEIN (TOP)

135   RICHARD FELBER (BOTTOM)

137   MICK HALES (TOP LEFT)

137   KEN DRUSE (TOP RIGHT, BOTTOM LEFT)

137   DANA HYDE (BOTTOM RIGHT)